HOPE VALLEY
THROUGH TIME
Dr Liam Clarke

AMBERLEY PUBLISHING

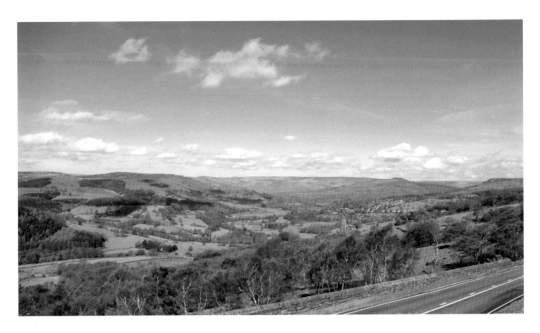

Hope Valley from Surprise View
This is the view from Surprise View. It shows Mam Tor in the distance with Win Hill and Losehill. The railway line that opened in 1894 can be seen in the valley.

First published 2012

Amberley Publishing
The Hill, Stroud
Gloucestershire, GL5 4EP

www.amberley-books.com

Copyright © Dr Liam Clarke, 2012

The right of Dr Liam Clarke to be identified as the Author of this work has been asserted in accordance with the Copyrights, Designs and Patents Act 1988.

ISBN 978 1 4456 0830 3

British Library Cataloguing in Publication Data.
A catalogue record for this book is available from the British Library.

Typeset in 9.5pt on 12pt Celeste.
Typesetting by Amberley Publishing.
Printed in the UK.

Introduction

About 300 million years ago much of the Hope Valley lay in a shallow lagoon surrounded by a deep sea teeming with plant and sea life. The oldest rocks in the area are limestone, formed around this time from the remains of the marine creatures that inhabited the sea and lagoon.

Half a million years ago the great ice age created many of the passes which shaped the present Hope Valley. Castleton, Hope, Edale, Brough and Bradwell were beneath a huge lake with two entries into it from the west, the Winnats and the gap between Mam Tor and Tray Cliff.

The first men to live in this area made their homes in the numerous caves that can still be seen in the valley and people have lived in these caves from the Bronze Age up until the eighteenth century.

Travelling has always been difficult in the Hope Valley. One of the earliest maps of the area does not show any roads or tracks in the Peak District. Moving about the valley was a very hazardous business as there were very few roads until the mid-seventeenth century. Even then these roads were either rudimentary or just tracks to individual farms or villages. Most of the roads were impassable because of snow in the winter and in spring they were subject to flooding as the snow melted.

Transport was by horse and packhorse, and was often easier on the high dry ground than on the lower mires and bogs of the Hope Valley. Travellers used the causeways on higher ground because the lower roads were so bad and were only passable in the summer months. Thomas Brown in 1662 commented that that the 'moor was such an uneven track of road, full of great holes, and at times swells with such rapid currents'. There is a network of track ways along the hills and down into the valley in all the Hope Valley villages. Some of them became sunken hollow ways worn down over the passage of time.

With the coming of the railway in 1894 the valley was opened up to tourists and commuters to Sheffield and Manchester. The railway also allowed industries to develop by facilitating easy access to markets.

For people living in the Hope Valley, agriculture has for many centuries been one of the chief forms of livelihood. Within the valleys there is considerable evidence for arable farming having taken place.

The Hope Valley has also had a number of industries which have operated at various periods. The earliest recorded are lead mining, corn milling, lime burning, cotton weaving, needle making, candle making and rope and twine making.

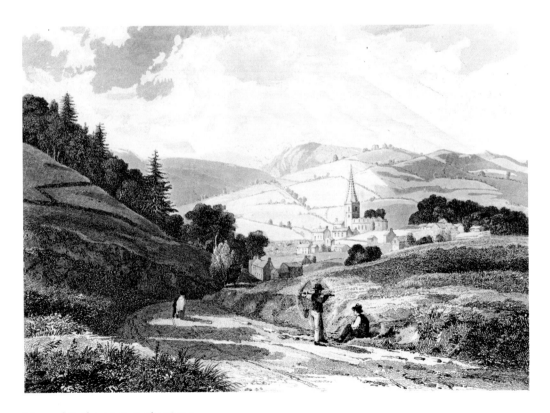

View of Hathersage, Early 1800s
This print of Hathersage was by Francis Chantrey in the early 1800s. It shows the route of the first turnpike road built in 1770 which followed an ancient track way into Hathersage from Sheffield. Hathersage church surrounded by old cottages can be seen on the hillside.

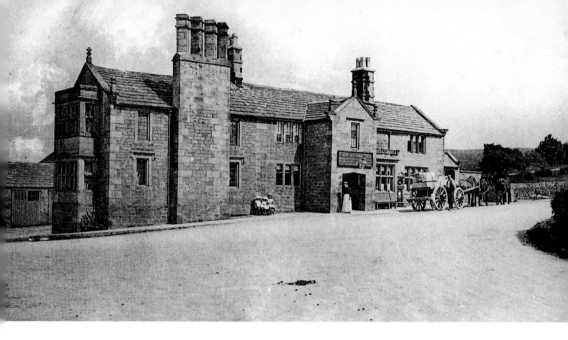

Fox House, Hathersage

This photograph is of the Fox House Inn in the 1890s when the inn keeper was John Thompson. It was built in 1399 by Nicholas Fox, rebuilt in 1773 and later extended as accommodation for the Duke of Rutland's visitors at his nearby shooting lodge at Longshaw. The building has changed little since it was used for the first horse change for coaches on the turnpike road opened in 1758. The stables at the rear of the inn are now hotel accommodation. This building was also the place where Charlotte Brontë's *Jane Eyre* reputedly was set down from her coach during her flight to Morton (Hathersage).

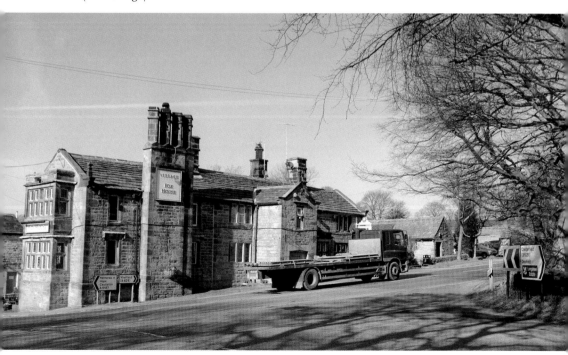

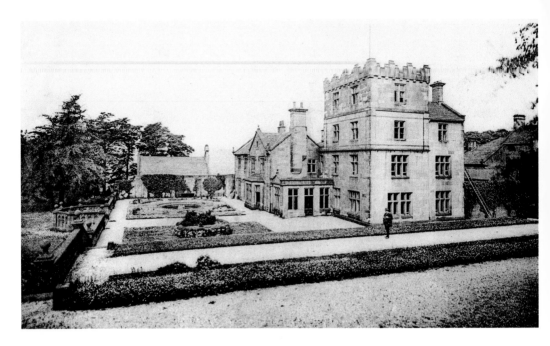

Longshaw Lodge

The late nineteenth-century photograph is of Longshaw Lodge built about 1830 as a shooting lodge for the Duke of Rutland to accommodate the large parties invited to shoot over his vast estate. Less important visitors stayed at the nearby Fox House Inn. The Lodge was used as an auxiliary hospital during the First World War. In 1931 the National Trust took over responsibility for the estate and it is now private accommodation.

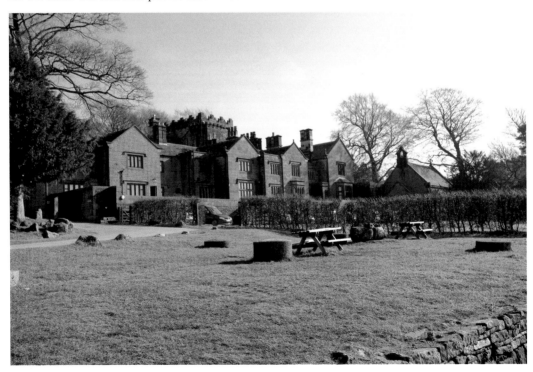

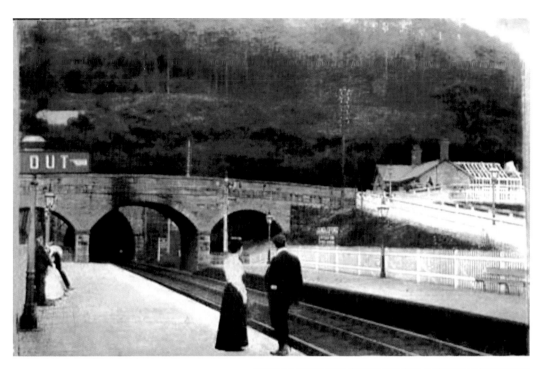

Grindleford Station

Grindleford Station was opened in 1894 on the Midland Railway's Dore and Chinley line at the western entrance to the Totley Tunnel. The line opened up the previously isolated Hope Valley to day-trippers and commuters from Sheffield. It was also used to transport stone from the local quarries. The station has much changed, it is now unmanned, the waiting rooms have disappeared and although the station building (being built in the 1894 photograph) is still in existence, it has become a popular café.

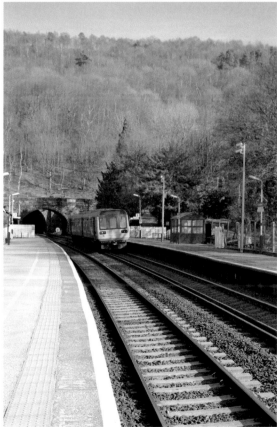

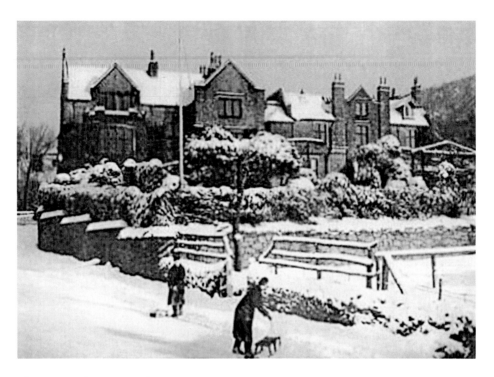

The Maynard Arms Hotel

The Maynard Arms Hotel, dating back over 100 years, still retains many of its period features. This winter scene shows how isolated this area of the Peak District can become for long periods in winter. Many times in the past villages were cut off by snow and bad weather. With the coming of the railway, Grindleford became more accessible and the area became a popular visitor attraction. Hotels sprang up all over the Peak District to accommodate tourists. The hotel building has changed very little over the years.

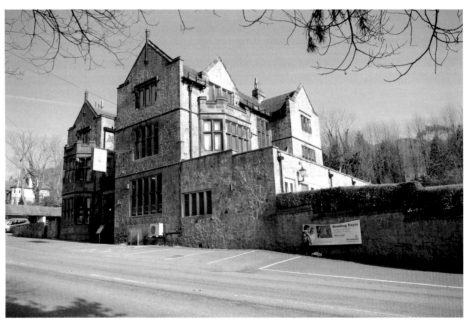

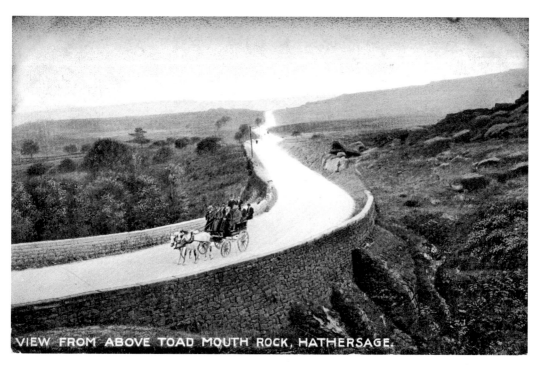

VIEW FROM ABOVE TOAD MOUTH ROCK, HATHERSAGE.

Toad's Mouth, Hathersage

Toad's Mouth is a natural boulder with additional carvings to make it resemble a toad. The 'Toad's Mouth Bridge' carries the main Sparrowpit turnpike road built in 1825 across Burbage Brook. This 1905 photograph shows a group of travellers returning to Sheffield after a day's outing in the Peak District. Note the few walkers on the road compared with the thousands who visit this part of Derbyshire today. Modern transport has opened up this area to visitors over the past 150 years.

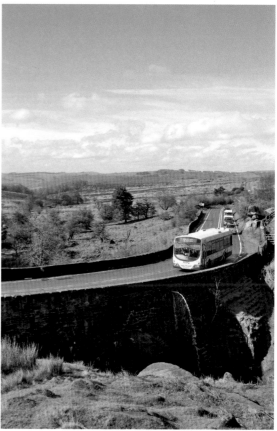

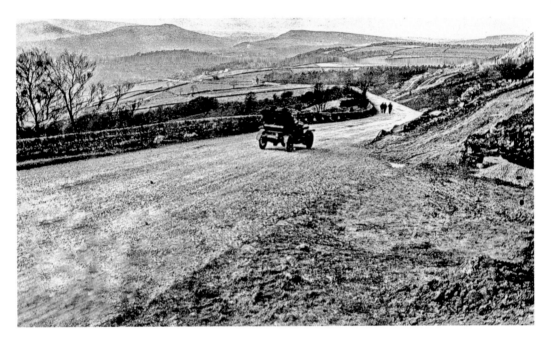

Surprise View, Hathersage

Surprise View is a unique view taking in the Derwent Valley, Hope Valley and the great ridge of Win Hill and Losehill. This photograph was taken from Millstone Edge, a gap made in the rocks to accommodate the Turnpike Road which was extended in 1825. On the right of the old 1910 photograph can be see a track way which led to a millstone quarry. This ceased production in the 1950s. The road is now busier but safer and has a pedestrian footpath.

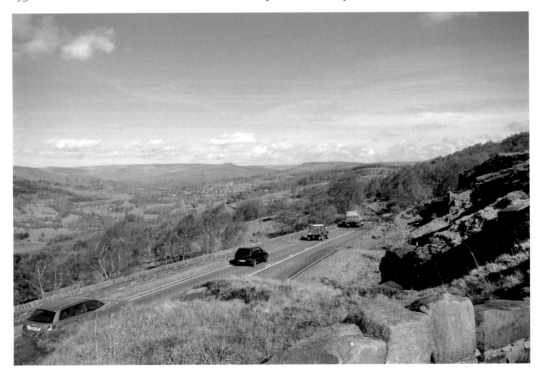

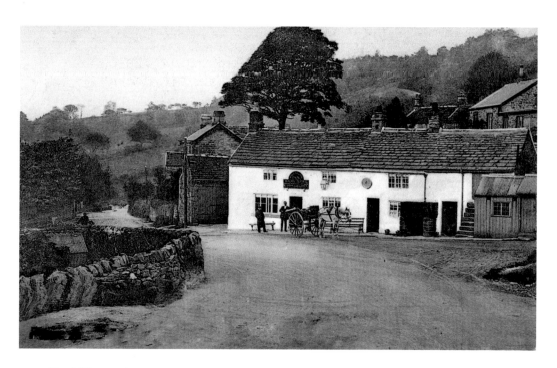

The Millstone Inn

The Millstone Inn originated as a farm house owned by the Eilkin family. After the Sheffield to Chapel-en-le Frith turnpike road was opened it became a licensed inn in the 1820s. In the 1890s William Eyre (a butcher) was the innkeeper. This old 1910 photograph shows the name of the licensee as Mary Eyre. The old inn was demolished in the late 1920s to be replaced with the present building.

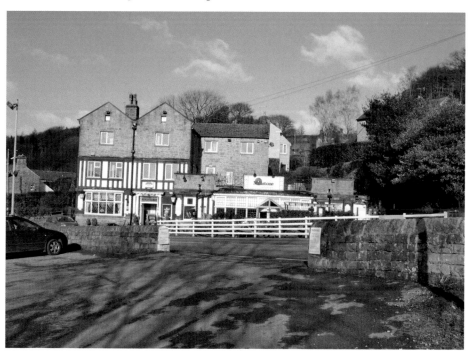

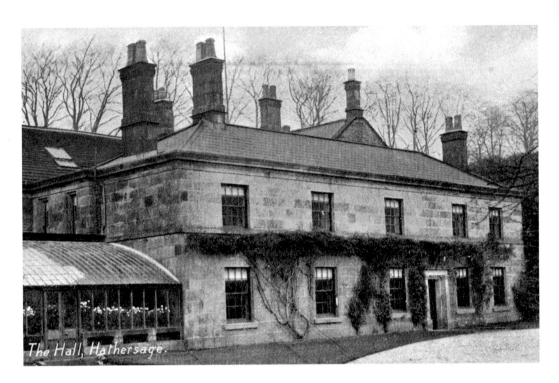

The Hall, Hathersage.

Hathersage Hall

This 1900 scene shows Hathersage Hall which dates from 1496. In the 1650s the Aston family transformed the original farmhouse into a gentleman's residence. The Hall was inherited by John Shuttleworth who had been a prisoner of war during the American War of Independence in late 1779. It underwent a major remodelling about 1830. The Shuttleworth family later moved to Nether Hall, a more peaceful part of Hathersage. The inset shows the malt kiln for the hall, now part of a business park.

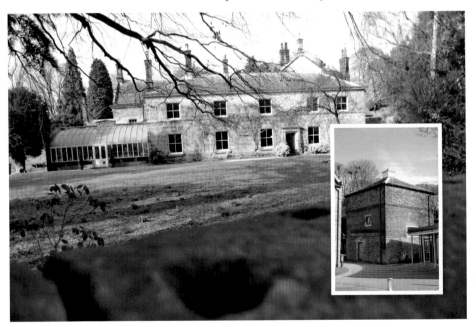

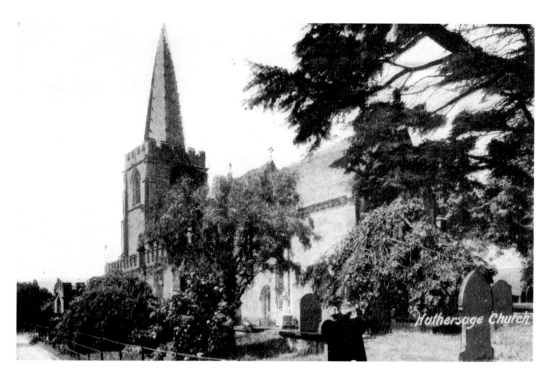

Hathersage Church

This photograph of Hathersage Church was taken in 1907. The ancient church of St Michael and All Angels was built before 1125. The church has a notable connection with Little John, a friend of Robin Hood who himself was thought to have been born eight miles away. Little John is believed to have been a native of Hathersage and to have been buried in a 10 foot long grave in the churchyard. In 1784 a 30-inch thigh bone was exhumed from the grave.

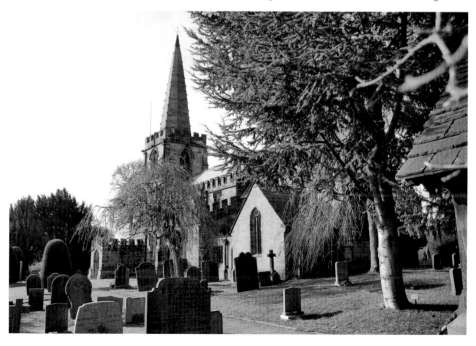

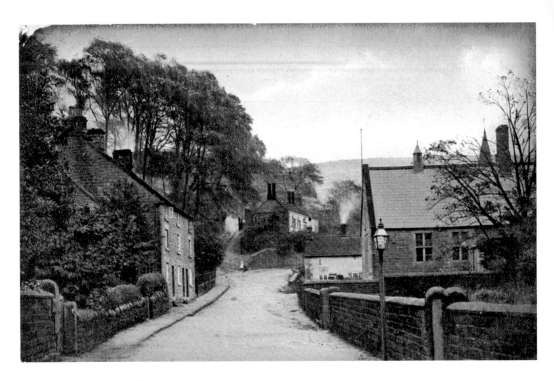

School Lane, Hathersage

This is a 1905 view of School Lane. It was the route of the first turnpike road built in 1770 and followed an ancient track way into Hathersage from Sheffield. After its construction it was possible for the first time to use carts and horses to bring commodities from Sheffield to Hathersage and the Hope Valley. On the right can be seen the first National School opened in the village in 1858. It is now the local primary school. Beyond the school is situated the Scotsman Pack, a hostelry which Little John is said to have frequented.

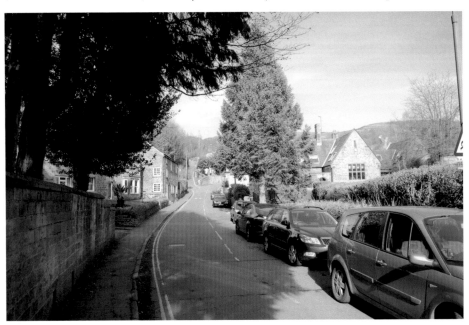

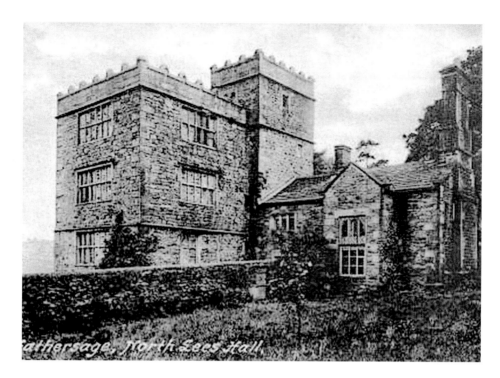

North Lees Hall

A house has stood on this site since 1306. It was occupied in 1551 by a noted recusant, Richard Fenton, who was convicted of being a Catholic in 1588 and died in prison. The present North Lees Hall was built in 1594 for William Jessop, a merchant from Sheffield. The building was later used as a paper mill which closed in 1887. This photograph shows the hall in the early 1900s. It is now owned by the Vivat Trust and is holiday accommodation. The Hall has become immortalised as 'Thornfield Hall' in *Jane Eyre* as the home of Mr Rochester and his unfortunate wife.

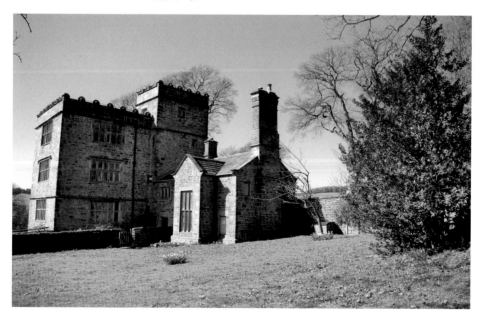

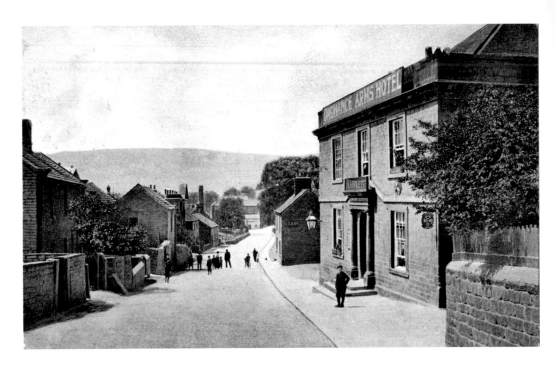

The Ordnance Arms, Hathersage

This is a scene about 1904 of the main street Hathersage. It shows The Ordnance Arms Inn on the right which was owned and opened in 1808 by Major Shuttleworth of Hathersage Hall. The name was changed to the Hathersage Inn in the 1960s and it is now an outdoor clothing shop. The building further down the road on the right is a bank replaced by a more modern building in 1909. The buildings on the left were once a farm and once a post office, owned by the Ibbotson family. They are now private houses. The tall chimney which can be seen was part of one of the needle mills in the village.

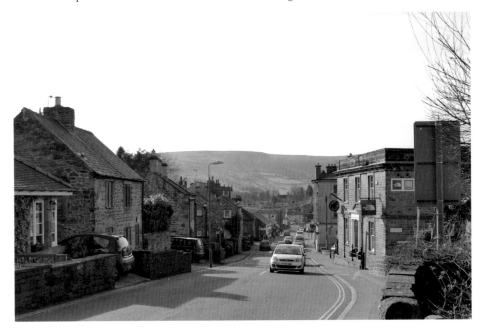

The Old Bank, Hathersage
This is a late nineteenth-century photograph of Hathersage High Street. The old bank built just after 1830 can clearly be seen. It was replaced in 1910 with a new building. At the bottom of the high street can be seen the chimney of the Atlas Works mill which was demolished in 1907. The building just in front of the mill is now a butcher's shop. All the trees and greenery have disappeared.

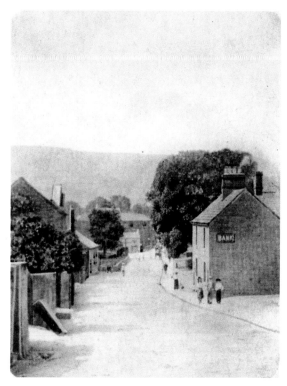

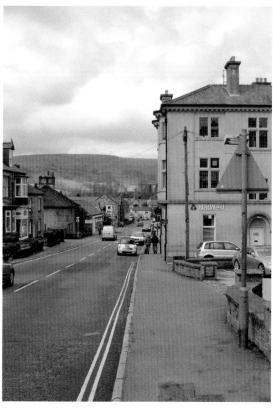

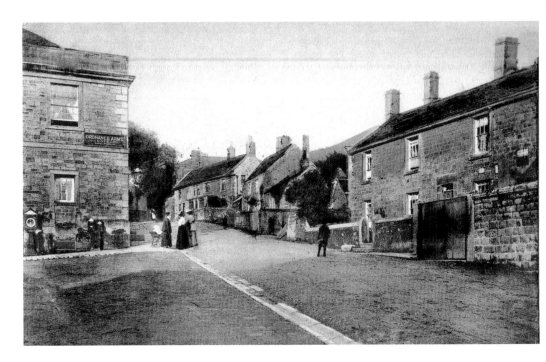

The Ibbotson Farm, Hathersage

This is a 1903 view of Hathersage High Street looking north. A number of Victorian ladies with their children are enjoying a conversation outside the Ordnance Arms Hotel. Note the farm building on the right, used as a post office in the mid 1800s, and the lack of footpaths. The gas lamp can clearly be seen on the wall of the Ordnance Arms Hotel. The open space on the left is now a car park for shops nearby. The scene looks much the same today but the road is much busier with traffic and visitors.

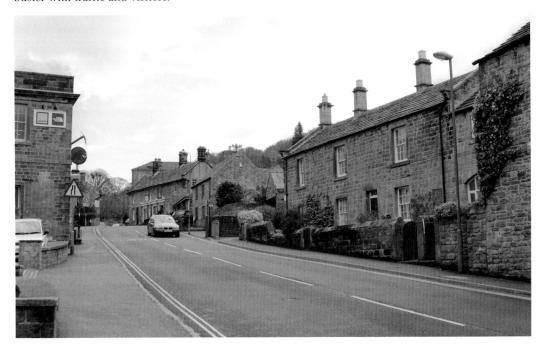

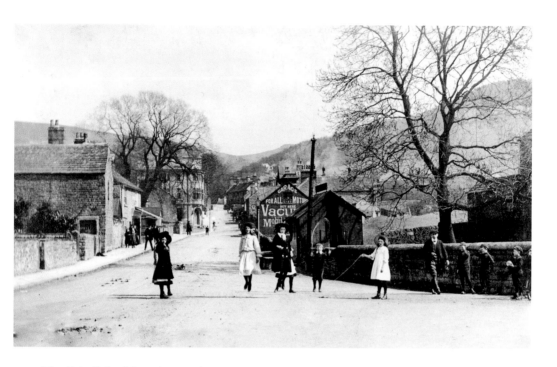

The Grindleford Junction, Hathersage

This 1910 scene gives some indication of how quiet and tranquil the main street in Hathersage was at the beginning of the twentieth century. Children play happily on the main thoroughfare. The gas lamps are still visible with gas supplied by The Hathersage & District Gas Company. This was situated where David Mellor's cutlery workshop stands today. Although few cars are in sight, the village had an automobile garage possibly where the present petrol station is situated today. The building on the left operated as a Hosier and Drapery shop in the 1920s. It is now the site of the Bank of Scotland. The hut behind the children would have been frequented often by them as it was a sweet shop for many years. Today this is a very busy road junction.

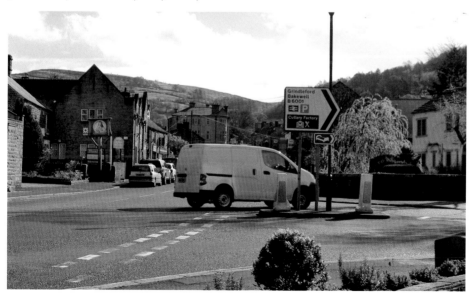

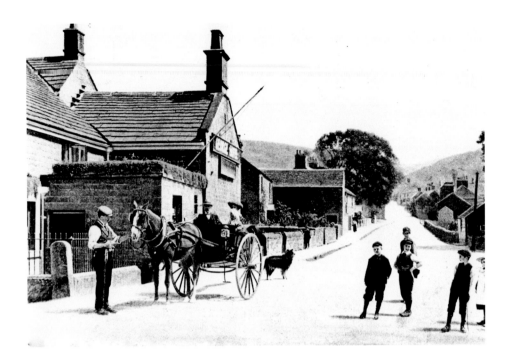

The George Hotel

This early 1900s scene shows the George Hotel built in the sixteenth century, originally called the St George and Dragon and situated on an important road junction. By 1835 it had become the George Inn and its landlord was George Morton. It functioned as a farmhouse, coach house and stabling for horses. When Charlotte Brontë first arrived in Hathersage on the stage coach she was met by George Morton. She later used his name for the village where Jane Eyre met Mr Rochester.

The house on the left has now been demolished and there are very few trees still standing in the vicinity of the main road today.

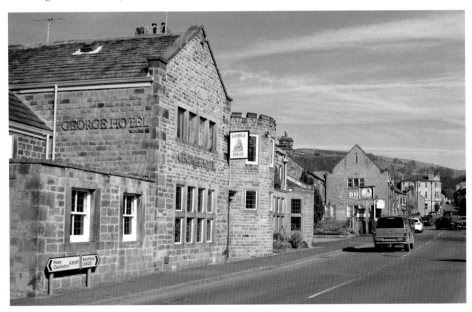

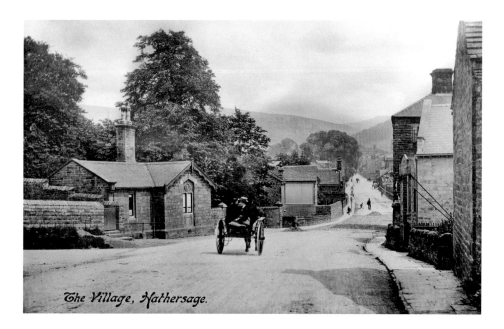

The Village, Hathersage.

Brookfield Manor Lodge

This early 1900s scene shows the Lodge to Brookfield Manor on the left by the junction with Jaggers Lane. Brookfield Manor has a date stone of 1656. The building was extended about 1825 when it was given a gothic facade. Brookfield Manor was 'Vale Hall' in *Jane Eyre*. The entrance to the Roman Catholic Chapel constructed in 1692, is also on the left just beyond the Brookfield Manor Lodge. This was the first Roman Catholic chapel to be built in England by public subscription after the Reformation. The building was ransacked shortly after construction and was not re-opened until 1806. The Wesleyan Institute was built on the site of the Atlas Works on the right of the photograph. It later became a Catholic Primary School and is now the Education Centre.

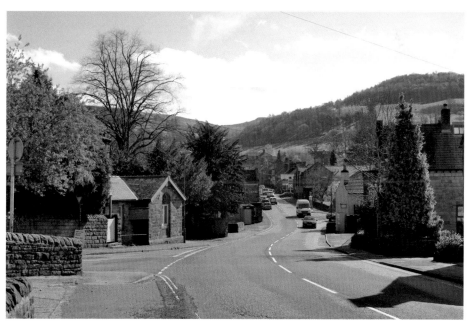

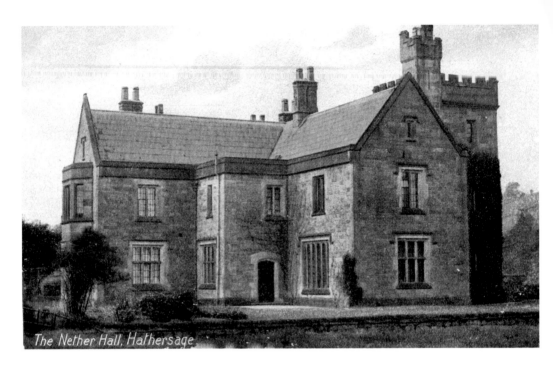

The Nether Hall, Hathersage

Nether Hall, Hathersage

This late nineteenth-century photograph shows Nether Hall built in 1840 by the Shuttleworth family when they moved from Hathersage Hall to a more peaceful and tranquil part of the village. John Shuttleworth had inherited the hall in about 1775. The new building incorporated the remains of an earlier seventeenth-century house. Except for the surrounding greenery, the house is very much the same today as when it was first built.

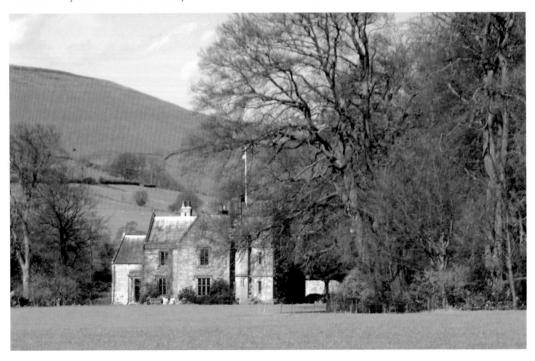

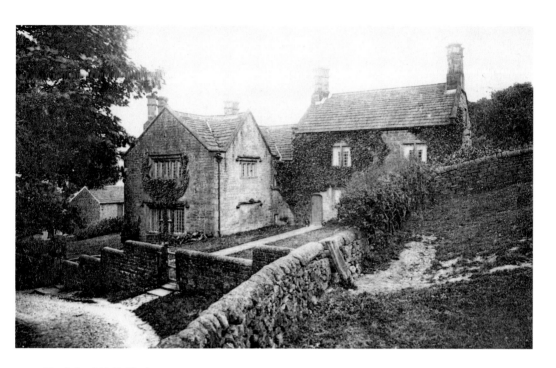

Hazleford Hall, Hathersage

Hazleford Hall is a beautiful old seventeenth-century building with mullioned windows on the lane from Leadmill Bridge just outside Hathersage. It was for a long time in the possession of the Padley family and later the Brushfield family. Little has changed since the early twentieth-century photograph was taken.

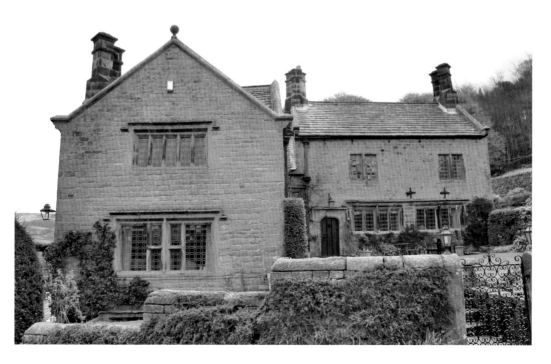

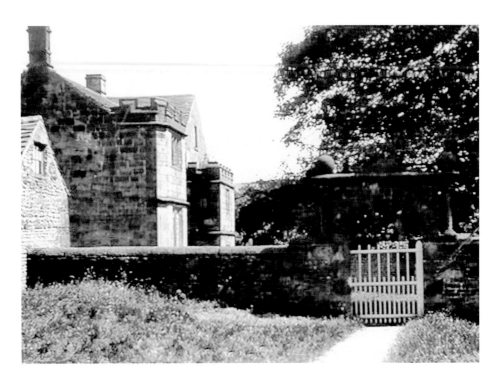

Highlow Hall, Hathersage

Highlow Hall is a historic manor owned by the Eyre family from approximately 1340 to 1842. The hall is associated with the white lady, a local ghost. The story recounts that in the 1300s Sir Nicholas Eyre courted the two sisters of the last male heir of the estate in the hope of gaining the property on his death. Sir Nicholas chose the eldest sister and the youngest was so distraught she disappeared from home. She later appeared to Sir Nicholas as a ghost stating that the Eyre family would eventually lose Highlow Hall. By 1843 the family were bankrupt and had to leave Highlow. The building has changed very little since the seventeenth century when the farm buildings were extended.

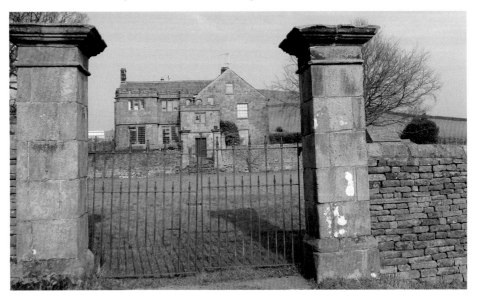

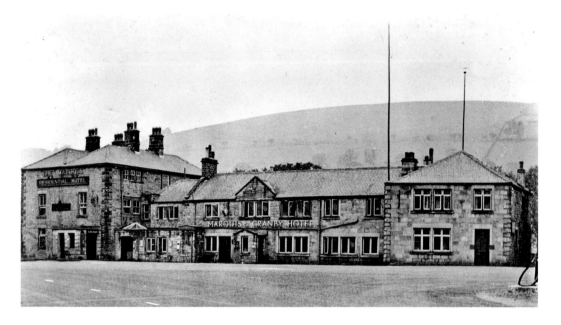

The Marquis of Granby Inn

This 1940s photograph shows The Marquis of Granby Inn which has been a land mark in the Hope Valley for many years. The earliest records indicate that the building was 'Sickleholme Farm' in 1842. By 1880 it had become Sickleholme public house and later in 1881 named the Marquis of Granby under the ownership of one James Belfield. Its position would indicate that it became a public house to service the travellers and tradesmen using the new turnpike roads. The old photograph gives an indication of the grandeur of the old building but it has been demolished and all that now stands is a derelict Victorian addition pictured in the modern photograph.

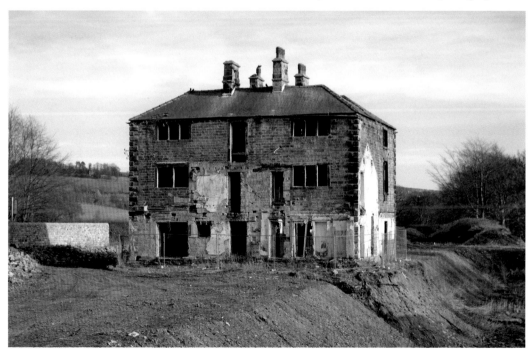

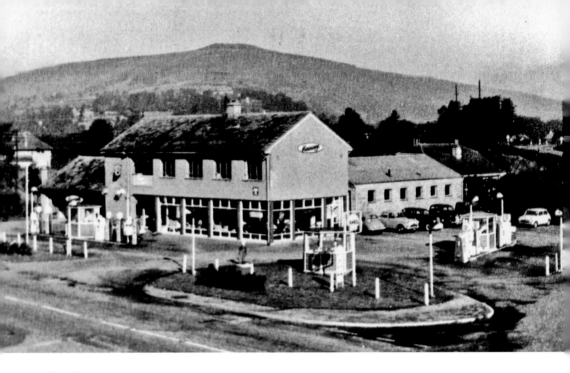

Sickleholme Garage

The Sickleholme Garage, like most businesses on this road, was developed to serve the needs of travellers on the new routes into the Peak District. This late 1950s photograph shows the property when it was Kennings Garage. Today the building at the side has been replaced with a car wash and the forecourt has been upgraded to meet modern requirements.

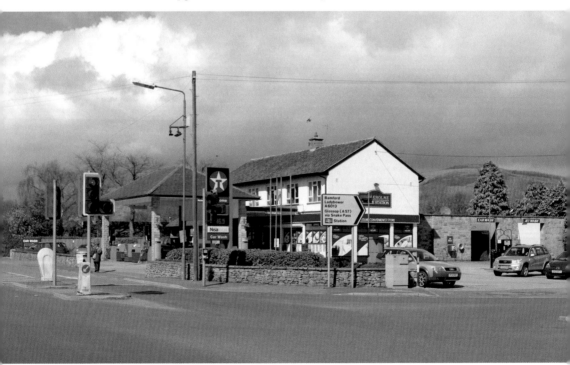

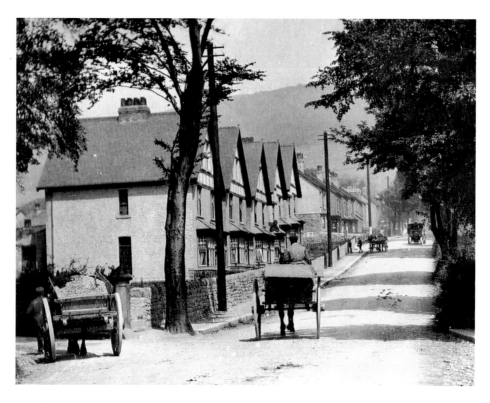

Bamford Mill Lane

This is an early 1900s scene of Bamford Main Road and Mill Lane. The horse and cart on the left is delivering coke to the gas works at Bamford Mill which produced coal gas used in the cotton spinning process. In the old photograph a passenger omnibus can be seen coming down the hill, possibly taking passengers to the local railway station. The main road and Mill Lane have been widened, the tree cut down but little else has changed.

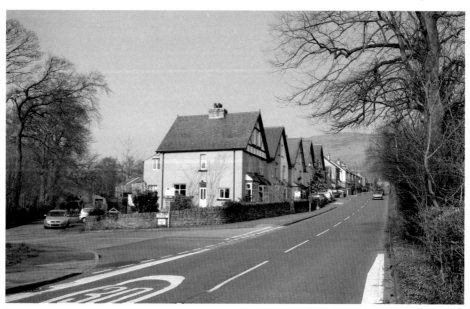

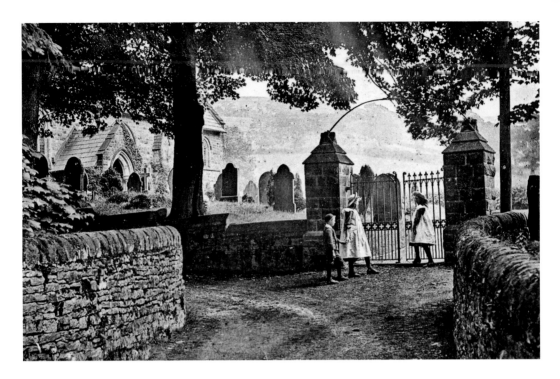

Derwent Churchyard

Derwent is a village 'drowned' under the Ladybower Reservoir. This scene shows children playing outside the churchyard in the late nineteenth century unaware that the village would later be flooded when the reservoir was completed in the 1940s. The later photograph is of the churchyard, fifty years later, screened off when the burials were being exhumed in 1940 to be re-interred in the village church at Bamford. Derwent church held its last service on 17 March 1943.

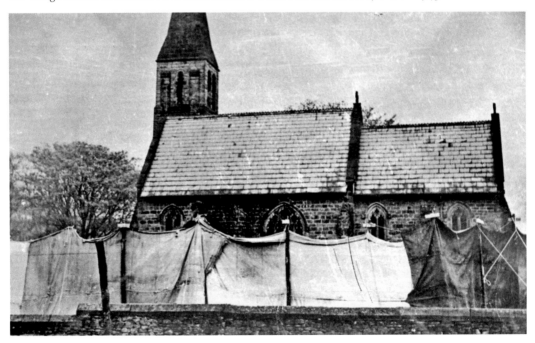

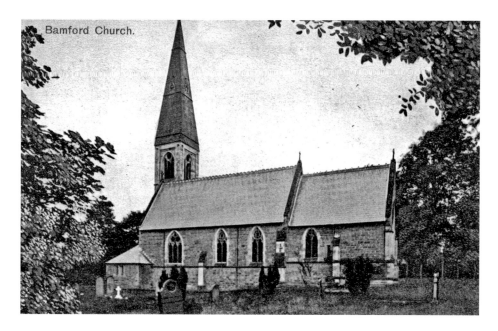

Bamford Church.

Bamford Parish Church

This photograph shows the parish church in the early twentieth century before the churchyard was extended to take the burials from nearby Derwent village. Bamford church was built in 1860 and designed by the famous Gothic Revival architect William Butterfield (1814–1900) who designed Keble College, Oxford and Rugby school's chapel and quadrangle in 1875. The church and rectory were paid for by Mr Moore, the owner of the local mill. Before the building of the church, people had to walk to the church at nearby Hathersage. The church remains much the same as when it was built. As can be seen from the later photograph only, the churchyard has been enlarged.

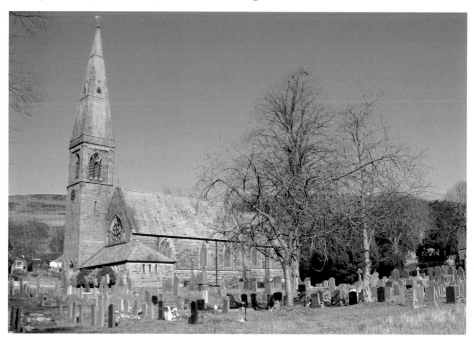

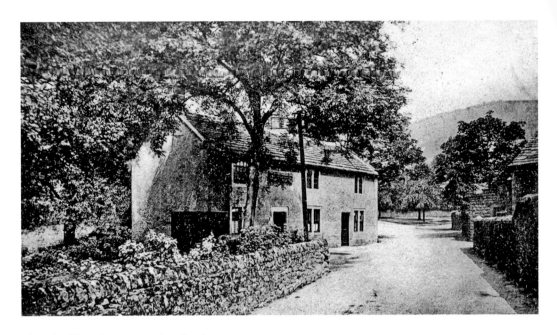

The Cheshire Cheese Inn, Bamford

This photograph is of the Cheshire Cheese Inn in the late nineteenth century. It originated as a farm. Like many others, beer was brewed here and it later became a pub. The Cheshire Cheese closed down in the beginning of the twentieth century, the licence being transferred to the pub across the road in 1902, now called the Angler's Rest. The building later became a butcher's shop and a bank. Part of the building was demolished to widen the road. It now serves as the local post office.

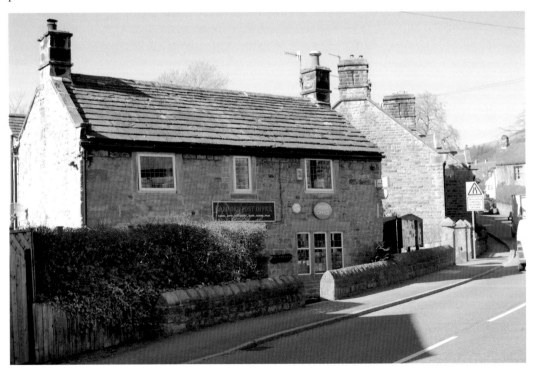

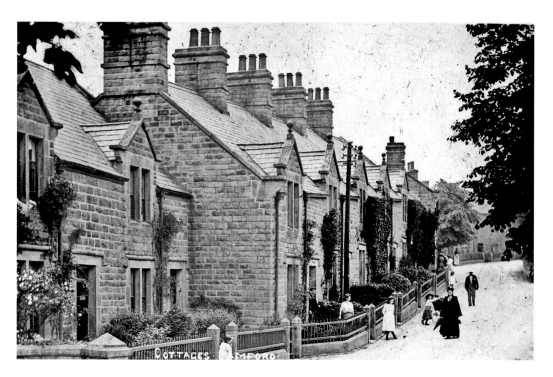

Post Office Row, Bamford

This 1910 scene shows the old Post Office Row, houses built in the late nineteenth century once known as Hollow Top. The doctor's surgery was at number 5 and the old post office was housed in number 4. Hollow Top was renamed Post Office Row after the post office moved to another location down the street. All the properties are now private housing. Little has changed structurally in the past 100 years but for the replacement windows installed to allow more light into the properties, and the removal of the iron railings during the war.

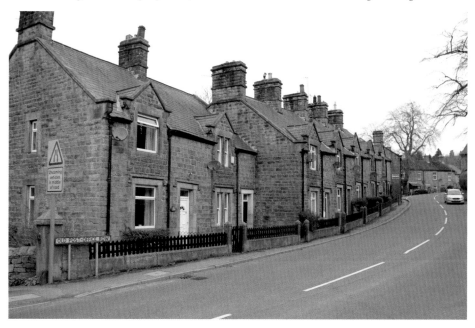

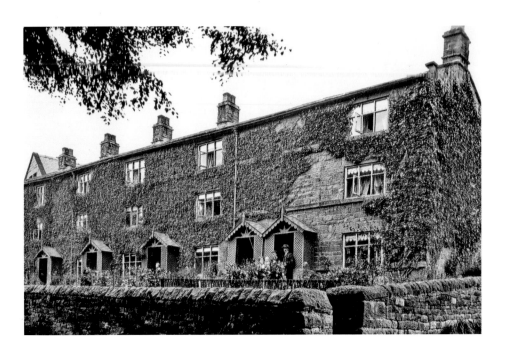

Greenhead Cottages, Bamford

This 1920s photograph shows Greenhead Cottages in the 1920s built to house weavers working in their own homes before the introduction of the large cotton mill in the village in the late 1700s. The weavers needed good light to carry out the weaving process at their looms and the large windows in the top floors of the building provided this. The cottages were probably built on this rise so that no shadows would block out the much needed light to the top windows. During the years little has changed in this corner of the village. The exteriors of the properties are very much the same as over 100 years ago.

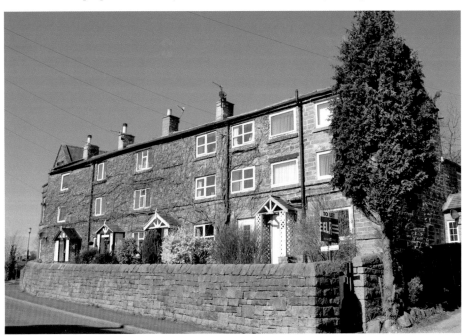

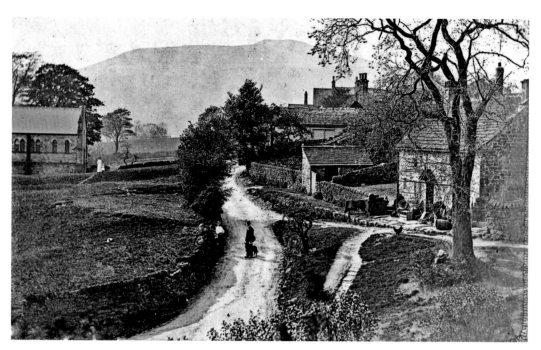

Taggs Knoll Bamford

This is a late nineteenth-century photograph of Taggs Knoll, a road named after a landlord of the Angler's Rest. The Catholic Church built in 1882, whose members include many relatives of the Irish men who worked on the building of the three dams during the beginning of the twentieth-century, is seen on the left. The fields on the left have been built over with housing which now obscures the view of the church. Both Taggs Knoll and the main road have been widened in the intervening years as seen in the later photograph.

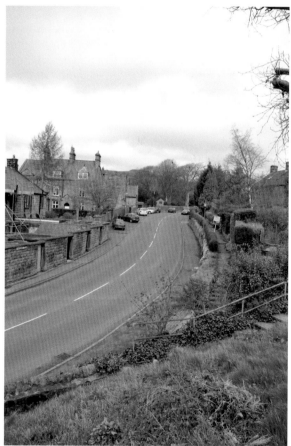

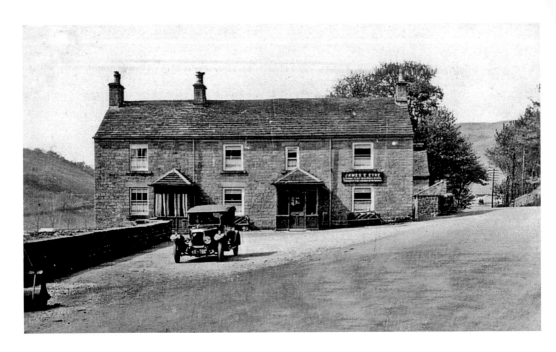

The Yorkshire Bridge Inn

The Yorkshire Bridge was the last crossing place over the Derwent River in medieval times before the Yorkshire border. The bridge was mentioned in 1599 as a wooden foot-bridge. In 1695 this structure was replaced by a new stone-built bridge to bear the weight of the packhorse teams who named it 'Yorkshire Bridge'. This early twentieth-century photograph shows the Yorkshire Bridge Inn whose licensee was James Eyre in the 1930s. The modern building has been much expanded but otherwise the scene is very much as it was eighty years ago.

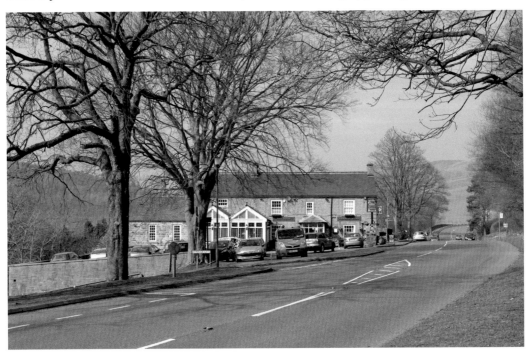

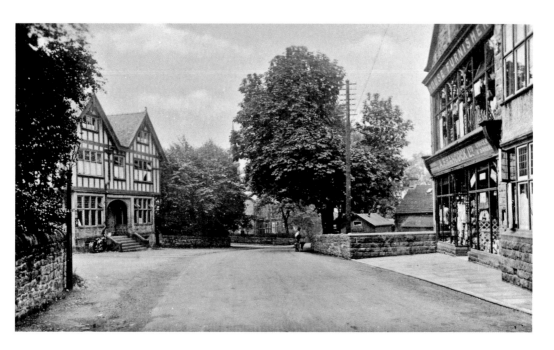

The Derwent Hotel, Bamford

This is a view is of the Derwent Hotel and Hancock's shop in 1915. Hancock's shop on the right of the photograph was a general store and headquarters of their business empire, which had expanded into many of the High Peak villages offering general provisions. The building is now a dental surgery. The Derwent Hotel is now closed and awaiting redevelopment.

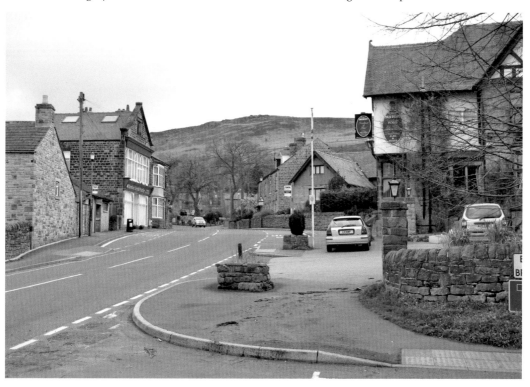

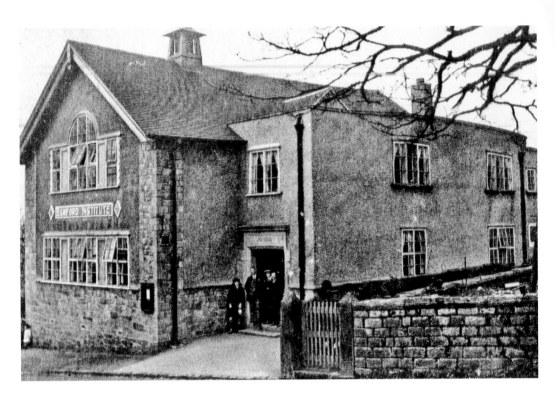

The Bamford Institute

This 1930s photograph is of the Bamford Institute, originally the Village Hall, built in 1912. The Institute, now the centre of activity in the village, is owned by the village and underwent refurbishment in 1999.

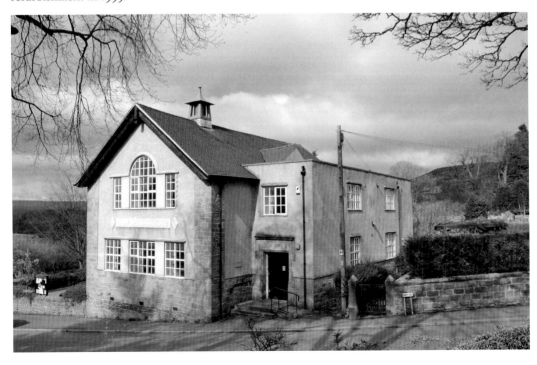

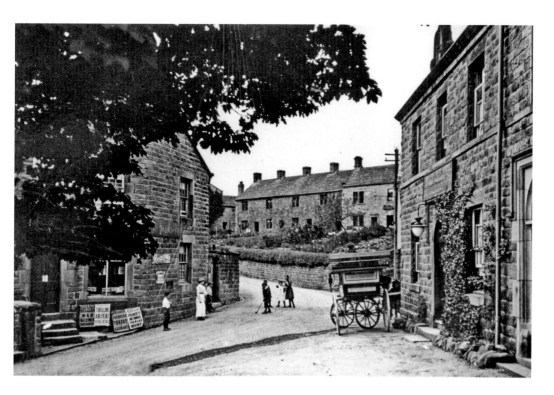

Angler's Rest and Greenhead Cottages

This picture taken in 1914 shows the Angler's Rest and Greenhead Cottages. The grocery shop on the left has newspaper boards with headlines from the *Daily Mirror*, 'Belgian War Scenes' and another telling of the 'Japanese Threat'. The young children in the street are playing golf. The scene has changed little today except for the usage of the buildings.

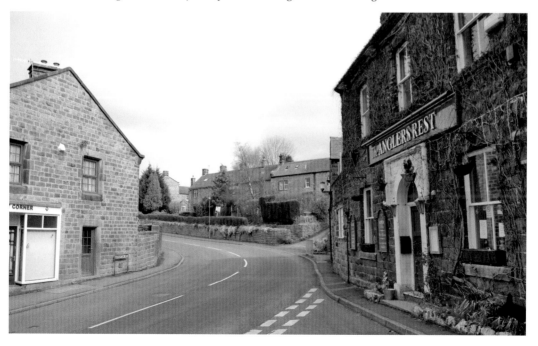

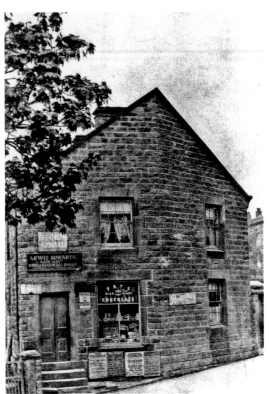

Quaint Corner, Bamford
This 1900s scene shows Quaint Corner, a newsagent, grocery and general dealer's shop. Advertisements in the window indicate that it sold 'Fry's High Class Chocolate'. The owner at the date of this picture was Lewis Rowarth. It was known as Top Shop and it later became an antique shop. It is now a private residence.

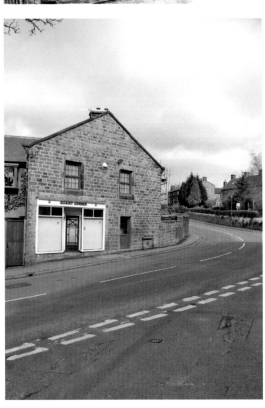

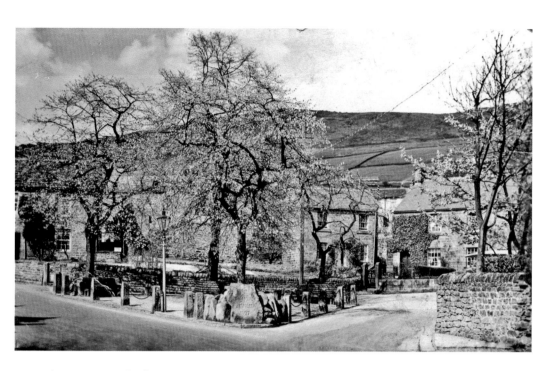

The Green Bamford

This is a mid twentieth-century photograph of The Green, Bamford. It is the centre for many activities in the village including the start of the annual carnival in July each year. The stone in the centre was set up to commemorate Queen Victoria's Diamond Jubilee 1897. Not much has changed except for the increase in greenery in front of the houses and the placement of a new stone commemorating the Diamond Jubilee of Queen Elizabeth II.

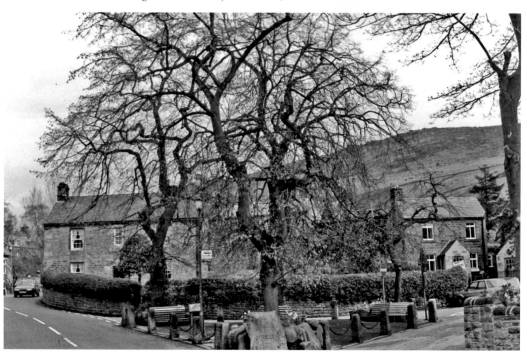

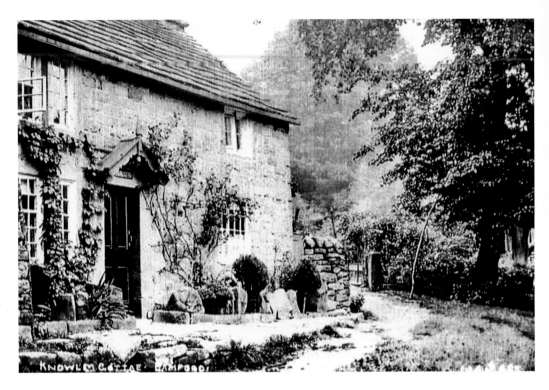

Knowle Cottage, Bamford

This photograph of Knowle Cottage, an ancient building, shows how rural parts of the village were in the late 1800s. No other houses are visible nearby at this date. Like many buildings in the village this one has later been extended and a porch added. The later photograph shows that a number of properties have been built nearby but are hidden by the trees.

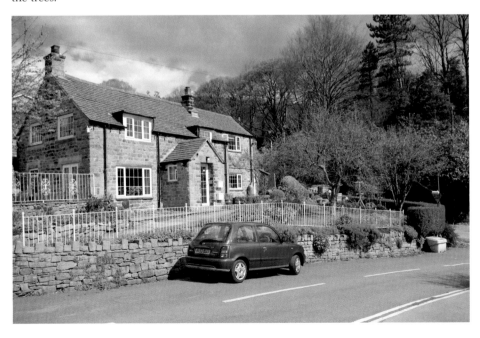

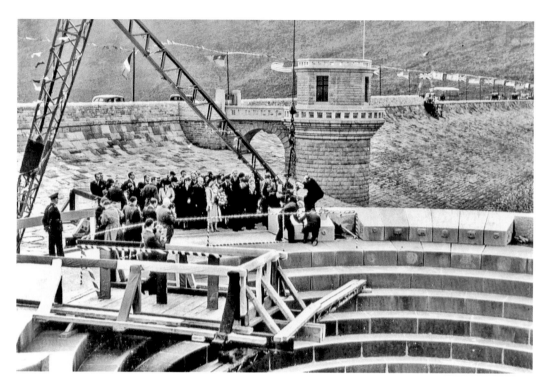

Ladybower Reservoir

This photograph was taken in 1945 showing the opening ceremony for the Ladybower Reservoir on Tuesday 25 September 1945 by King George VI accompanied by the future Queen Elizabeth. Ladybower was built between 1935 and 1943 by the Derwent Valley Water Board, and it took a further two years to fill. The building of the dam required the flooding of two nearby villages Derwent and Ashopton. The reservoir now supplies water to Sheffield and other midland cities.

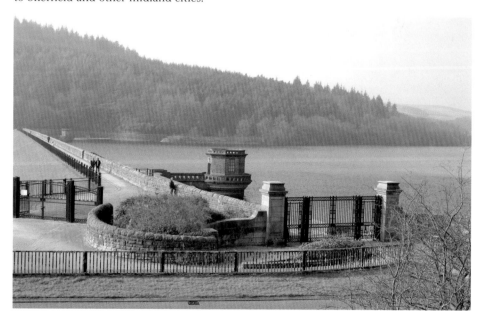

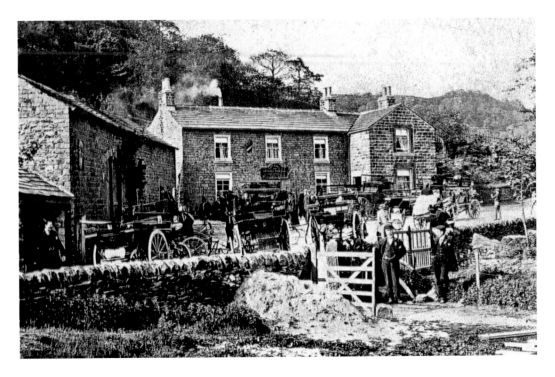

The Ladybower Inn

This was obviously a very popular inn in the late 1800s as this scene shows. The photograph is of some form of outing. Note the many different forms of transport outside the inn. The inn overlooks the modern reservoir and still offers accommodation and meals. The stables have been converted to accommodation but the main building looks very much as it did in the 1800s.

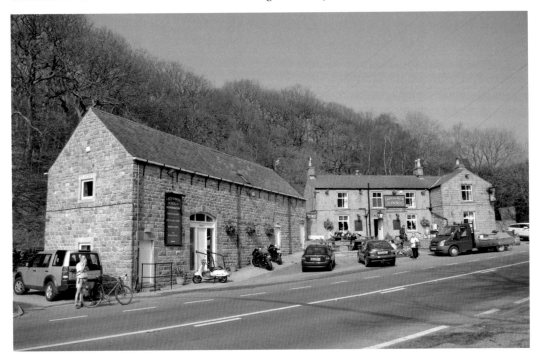

Derwent Village

This photograph is of the village of Derwent in the early 1900s before the building of the Ladybower reservoir. Derwent village was a small collection of stone dwellings and out-buildings clustered around a narrow winding street. The later picture, taken some time in 1944, shows the village just a year before it would be completely flooded by the rising waters of the reservoir. The houses have been vacated and the churchyard has no grave stones as all the burials have been moved to nearby Bamford churchyard.

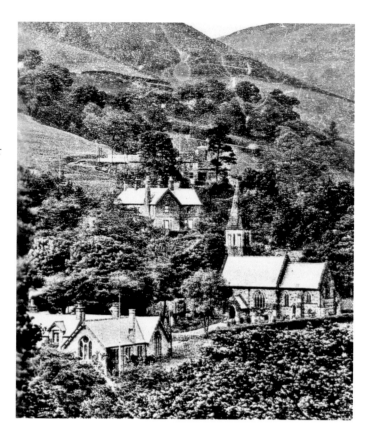

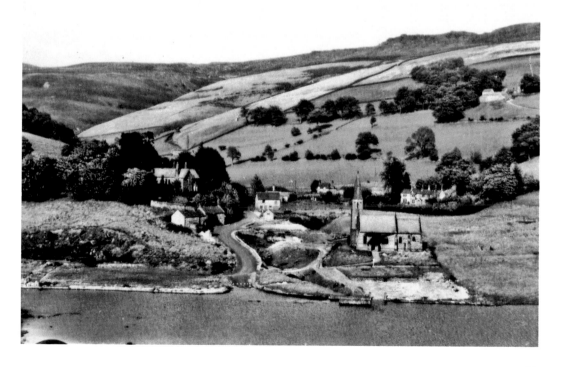

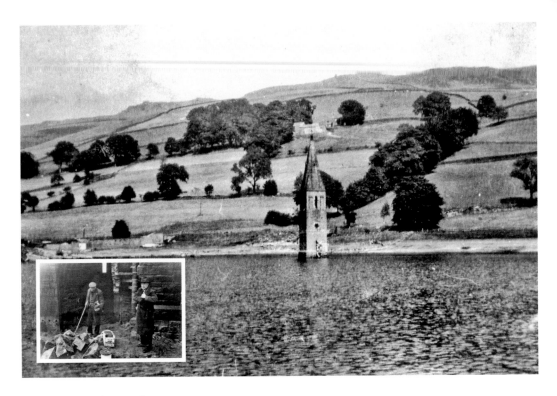

Derwent Church Steeple

This photograph shows the steeple of Derwent church, taken in the late 1940s, before it was blown up in 15 December 1947. It was possibly removed to stop people trying to swim to it. The inset shows the demolition men getting ready to blow up the steeple. Today the steeple can no longer be seen.

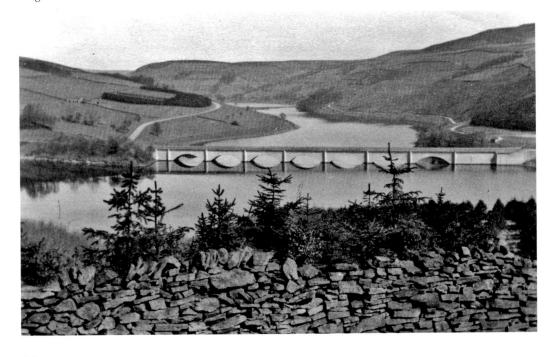

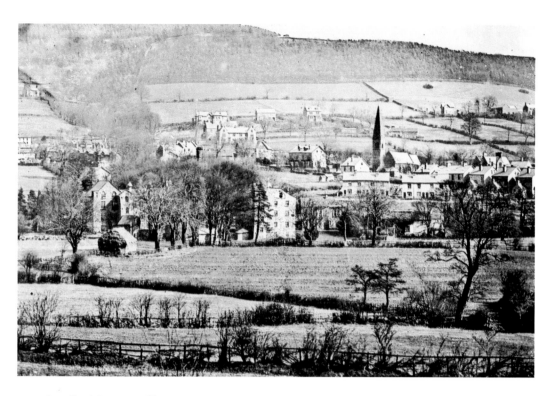

Bamford Cotton Mill

This pre 1900 photograph shows the Bamford cotton mill built on the site of an earlier corn mill. It operated from 1782 but was destroyed by fire in 1791 to be later rebuilt by Mr Moore, a benefactor to the village. It went through many hands before the chimney was demolished in 1966 and the buildings converted into residential accommodation.

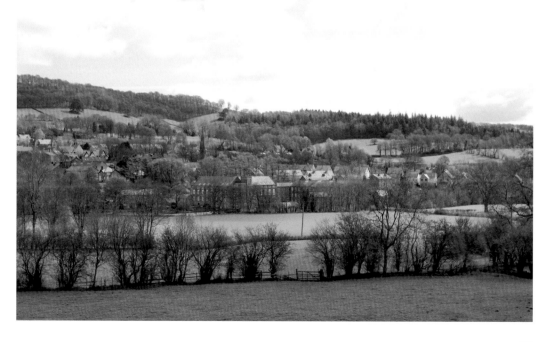

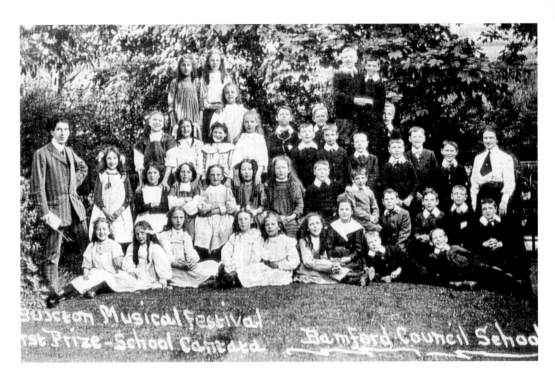

Bamford School

This late 1800s photograph is of Bamford Council School children who had taken part in the Buxton Musical Festival and won first prize. The children and staff look very pleased with their efforts. The school is still in existence now as Bamford Primary School.

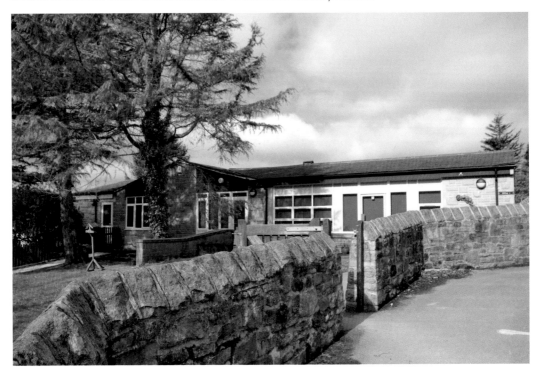

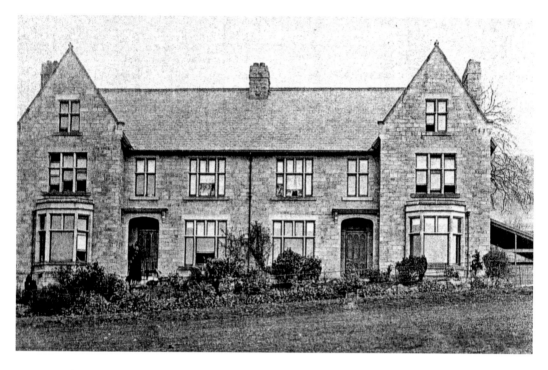

Bamford (Derwent) Grammar School

This is an early twentieth-century photograph of the Derwent Grammar School at Bamford, also called the Bamford Grammar School. The structure of the building has not changed in the intervening 100 years but is now private accommodation.

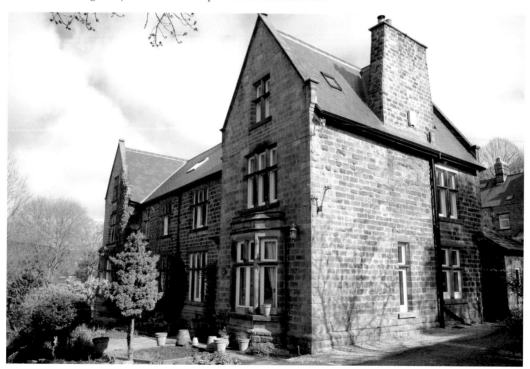

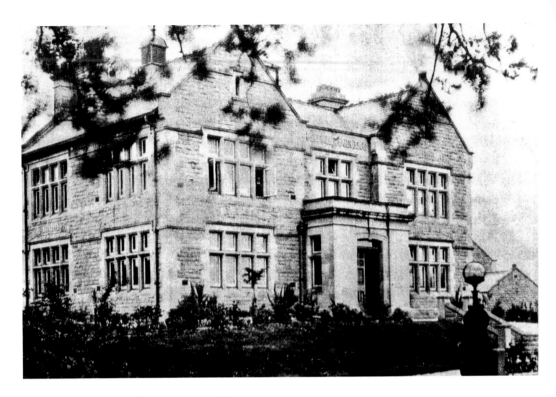

The Derwent Valley Water Board

The Derwent Valley Water Board was set up in 1899 to enable a supply of water to the cities of Derby, Nottingham and Sheffield and the county of Derbyshire from a series of reservoirs along the upper reaches of the River Derwent. It was disbanded in 1974. These photographs show the Board's headquarters in Bamford, now a Quaker Centre. The inset shows some of the water board employees in the early twentieth century.

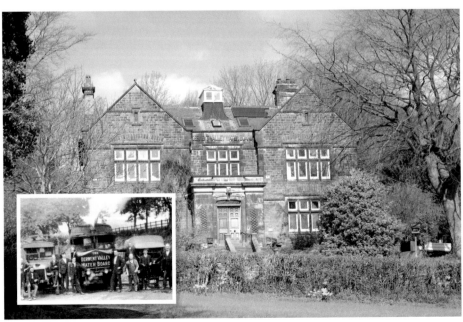

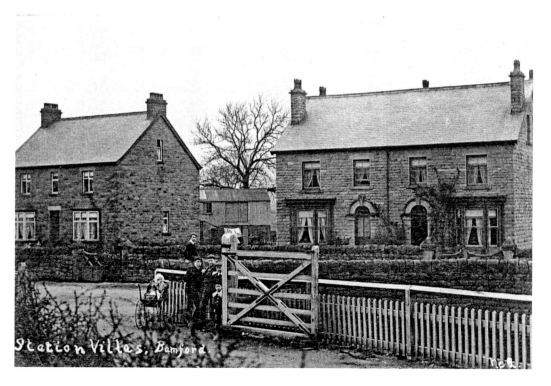

Station Villas, Bamford

This 1910 photograph shows houses on Station Villas built for the local railway employees. Some boys are posing for the photographer at the gate to the railway station. Bamford station still exists but is unmanned and many of the old buildings have been demolished.

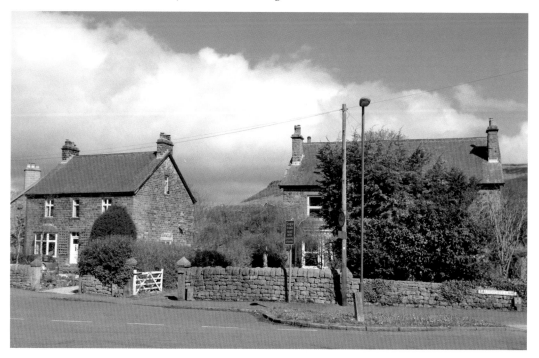

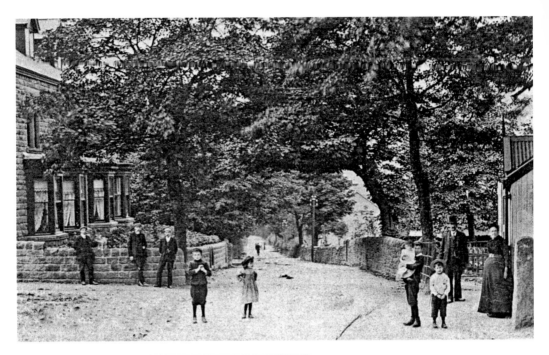

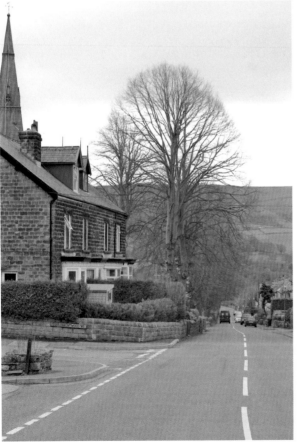

Bamford Main Road

This photograph shows the main road running south through Bamford in the early 1900s.

The road was very narrow and overshadowed by large trees a few of which remain today. The houses on the left have not changed and the wall still exists but all the walls and trees on the right hand side of the road have disappeared and a footpath has been made.

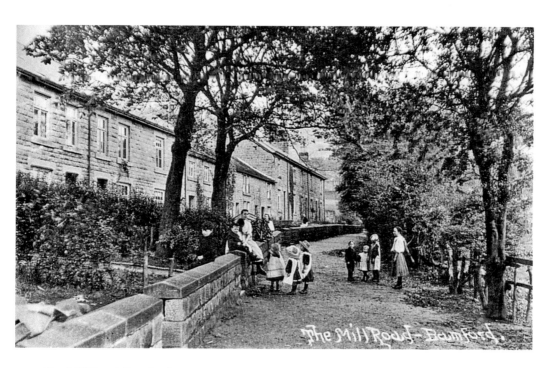

The Mill Road, Bamford

This is the original road that passed through the village and was part of the old Mortimer Toll Road. The wheels of drovers' carts hollowed out part of the road which is now called The Hollow. Many of the gardens in front of the houses have overgrown and the road has been widened in the intervening years.

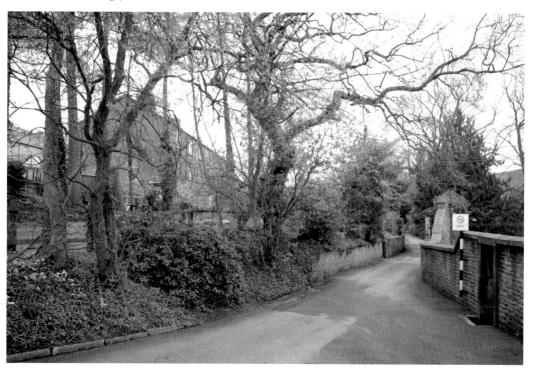

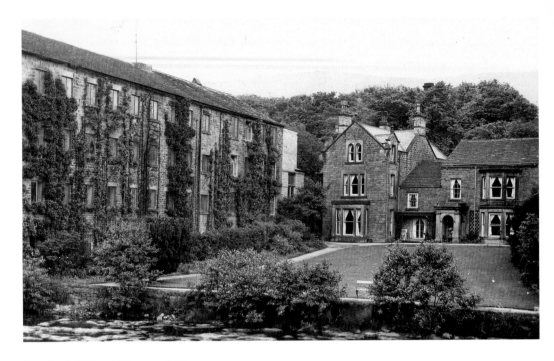

Bamford Mill and Manager's House

This picture of Bamford Mill and the manager's house was taken in 1920 when it was still a working mill. It is not possible to take a similar picture today. The later photograph shows the entrance to the manager's house which is now private accommodation. The property on the left was the old gas works which served the mill in the cotton spinning process.

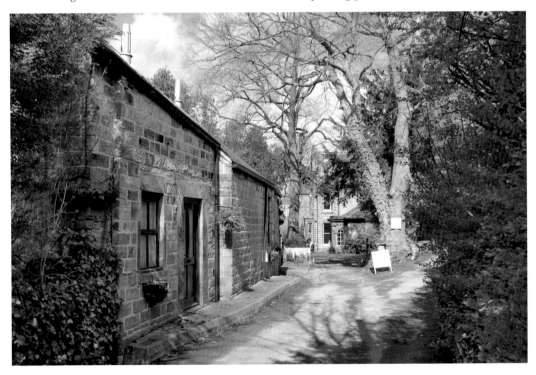

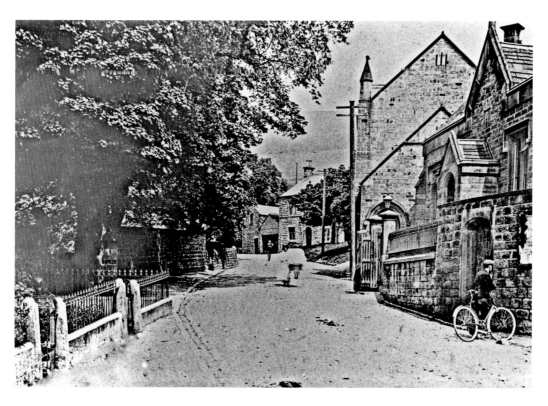

New Wesleyan Chapel, Bamford
This is a 1915 photograph of the New Wesleyan Chapel opened in 1890. This replaced a single-storey building of 1821. The construction of the new chapel began in 1889. It was extended in 1908 when gas lights were installed. Electricity followed in 1935. It boasted a Sunday School, Band of Hope, Girl Guides and a choir. The building is still in use today.

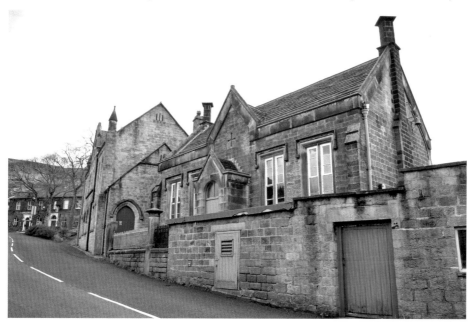

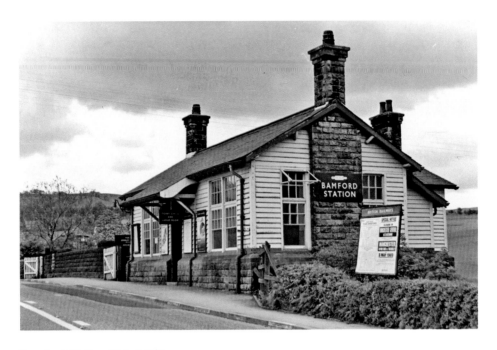

Bamford Station Ticket Office

Bamford Station was built by the Dore & Chinley Railway and was opened for goods traffic on 6 November 1893 and for passengers in June 1894. This is a photograph taken in 1968 of the old ticket office and ladies' room opened in 1895. The station became an unstaffed halt in 1969 when the last station master purchased the Station House. The main station building was located on the road bridge over the railway line. The building was removed during the late 1970s. The modern picture shows the present station and in the background can be seen the old station master's house, now a private residence.

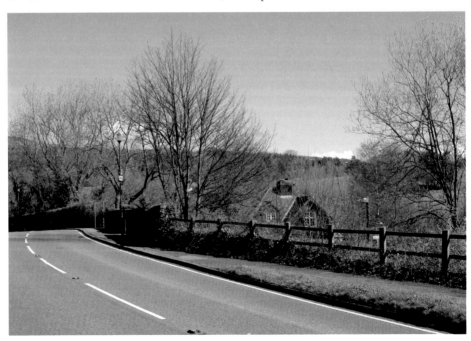

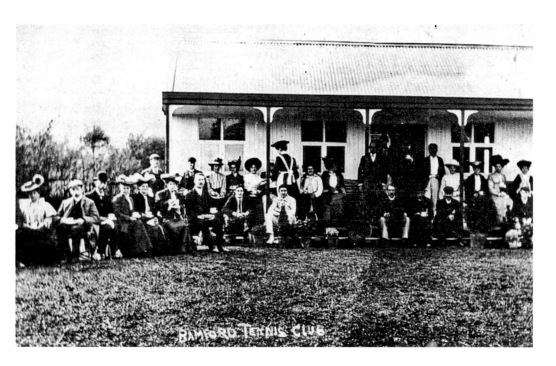

Bamford Tennis Club

This late Victorian photograph shows the Bamford Tennis club members outside their new clubhouse being served tea and cakes. The building is still standing but is no longer used as the tennis clubhouse. The modern photograph shows the present tennis courts and clubhouse.

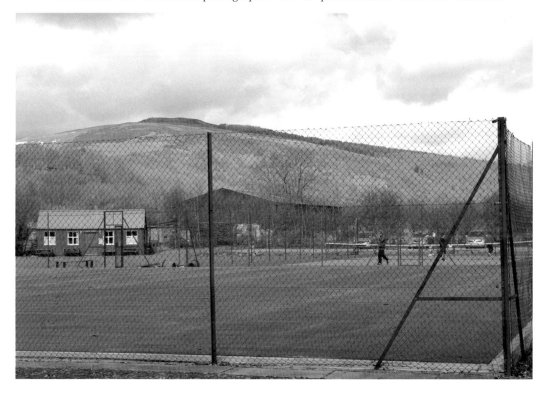

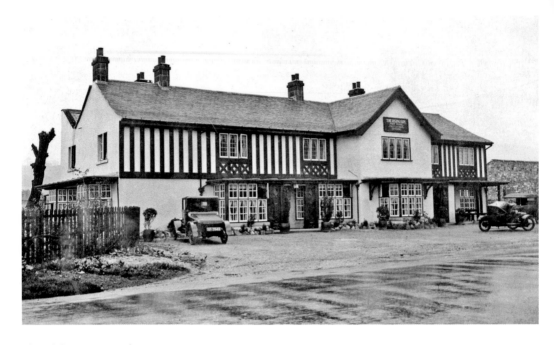

The Rising Sun Hotel

This 1930s photograph is of the very well known eighteenth-century land mark of the Hope Valley. The building is much the same today but for some extensions and a more defined car park.

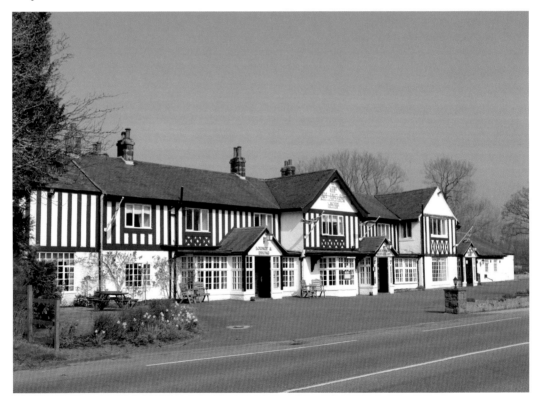

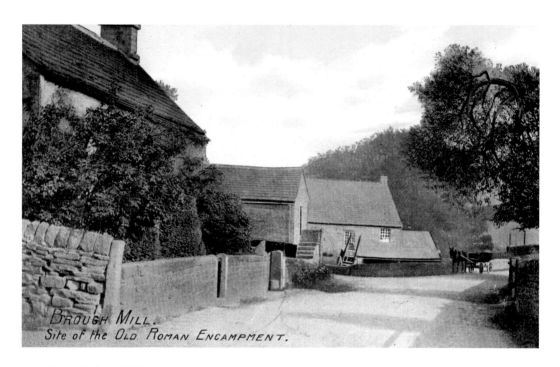

BROUGH MILL.
Site of the OLD ROMAN ENCAMPMENT.

Brough Corn Mill

This is a photograph taken in 1905 of Brough Corn Mill first mentioned in 1199 when it was assessed to the value of £4 per annum. It had been in the Eyre family since 1625. Later in 1885, another branch of the Eyre Family, William Eyre, formerly a joiner and wheelwright, took over the lease of the mill later buying it in 1911. There were also three other cotton mills in the local vicinity. The Eyre's mill still exists today as an agricultural merchant's.

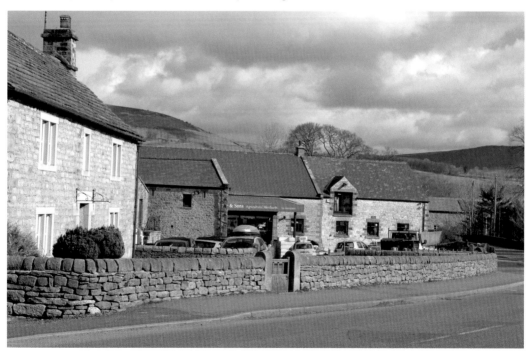

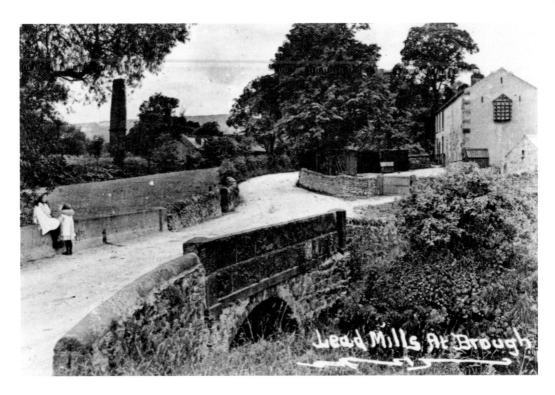

The White Lead Mills, Brough

This photograph is of the White Lead Mills at Brough in 1900. They began life as a cotton mill and later a white lead mill operated by the Ashton family. Lead smelting was carried out twenty-four hours a day. Production ended in 1924, but remnants of the cotton mill can still be seen. It is a business park today with a number of small firms operating. The chimney of another lead works, demolished in 1949, can be seen on the left of the old photograph.

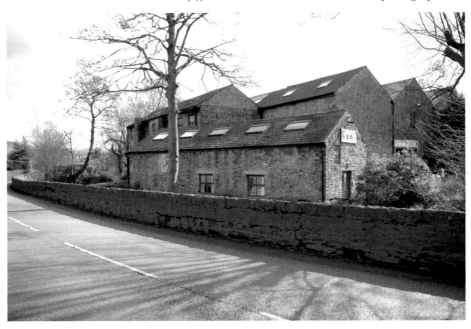

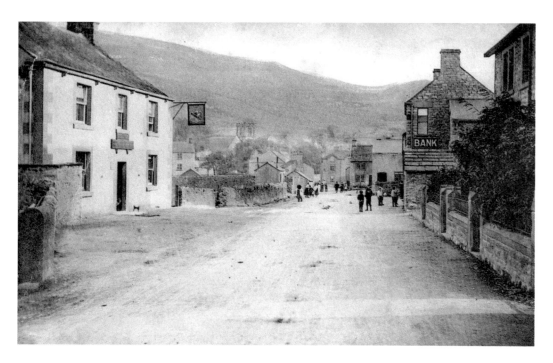

Netherside Bradwell

This scene of Bradwell High Street shows the Newburgh Arms Inn and local bank in 1910, which is long gone and was once the Crompton and Evans bank. The inn is now private accommodation. Many of the open spaces have been in-filled by buildings. Footpaths have been created to allow pedestrians to walk safely along, what is now, a very busy main road. The church can be seen in the background.

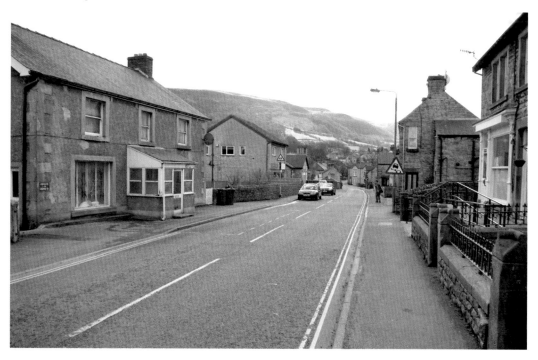

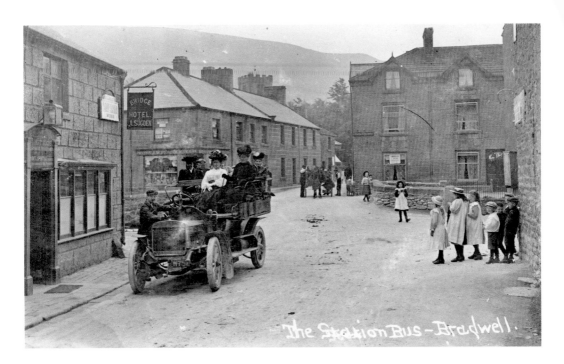

The Station Bus, Bradwell

This photograph shows passengers on the Station Bus, Bradwell which would take them to the nearby Hope Station in 1910 for onward travel to Sheffield or Manchester. In 1891 John Fox, farmer and omnibus proprietor, ran a service. By the time of this photograph, the service ran on a regular basis from the Bridge Hotel run by A. Sugden. Peacock's shop can be seen just over the bridge. Behind the bus can be seen men delivering coal by horse and cart. The hotel is now residential property and the bus for Sheffield or Castleton runs along this route today.

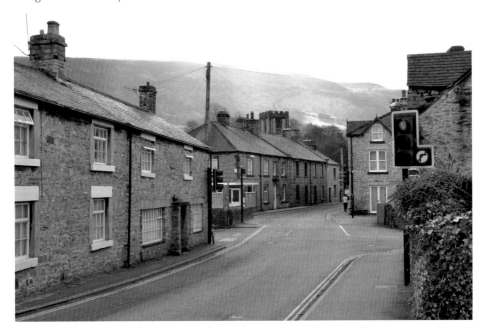

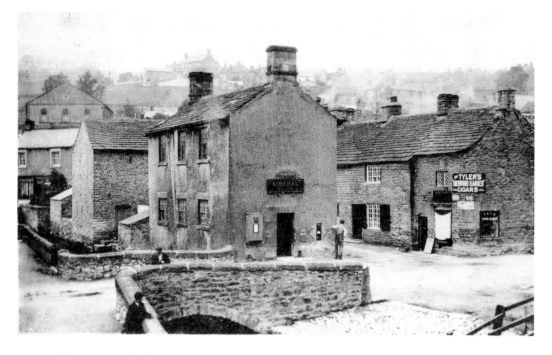

Bridge End Bradwell

This photograph of Bridge End Bradwell was taken about 1910. It shows the Liberal Club and the corner shop advertising 'Tylers Sherwood Ranger Cigars'. A cover is seen over one of the shop windows to keep the sun off the merchandise. Notice the window shutters on the property next to the shop. The shop today is Bradwell Ice Cream established in 1899 in the village. The large building was a Liberal Club, it is now private residence and once was a Wesleyan Sunday School.

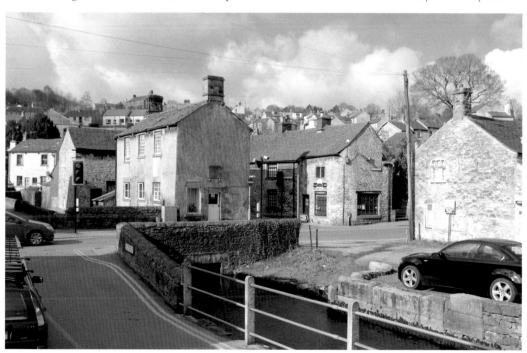

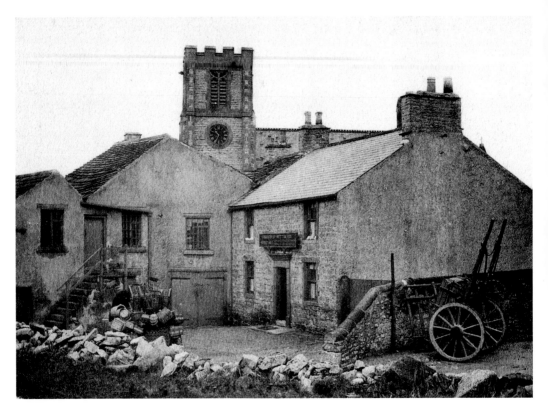

The Shoulder of Mutton Public House, Bradwell

This is a 1903 picture of the Shoulder of Mutton public house. The licensee in 1891 was Mrs Harriet Hall. The last landlords were the Boulton family who took over the new Shoulder of Mutton pub when the old pub closed. The old pub is now residential property and the new pub is situated on the other side of the busy main road.

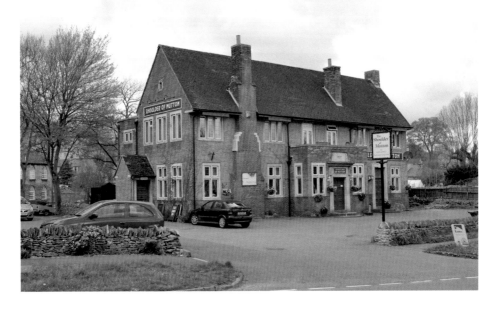

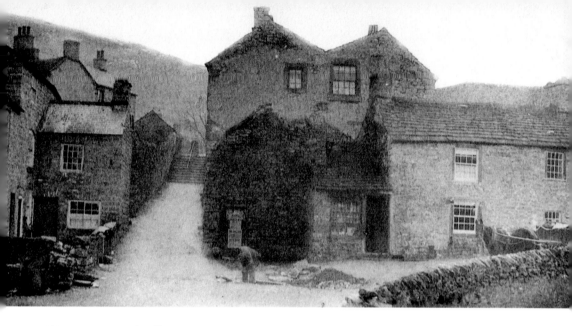

Water Lane, Bradwell

This early twentieth-century photograph of Water Lane Bradwell shows unplanned building development over years which created a beautiful atmospheric spot. The modern photograph shows that some building continued until recently but the area has changed very little over the years.

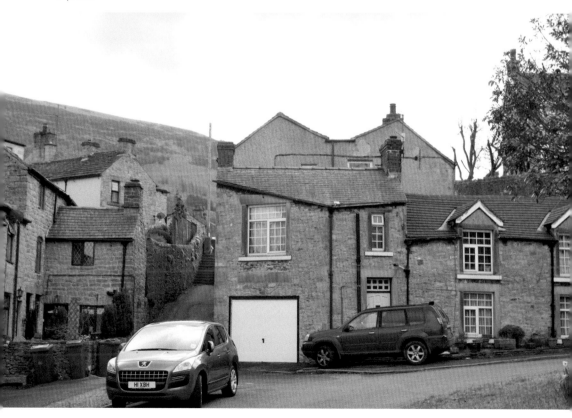

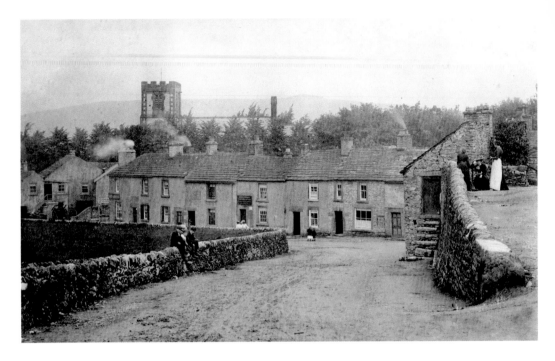

Dale End, Bradwell

Another quaint corner of Bradwell in the early twentieth century. The young boys sitting on the wall seem to be enjoying the photographer's attempt to capture the scene. The ladies on the right are in their Victorian finery for the occasion. The modern scene is much the same except for parked cars and the area on the left is now a garden.

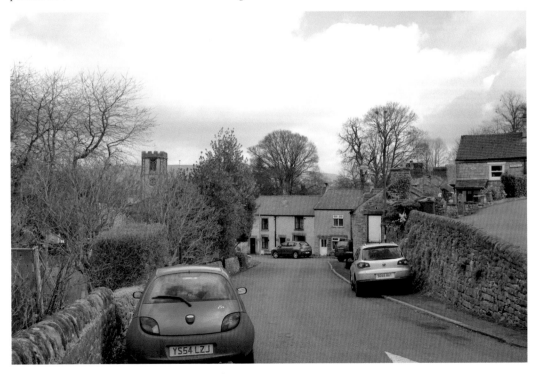

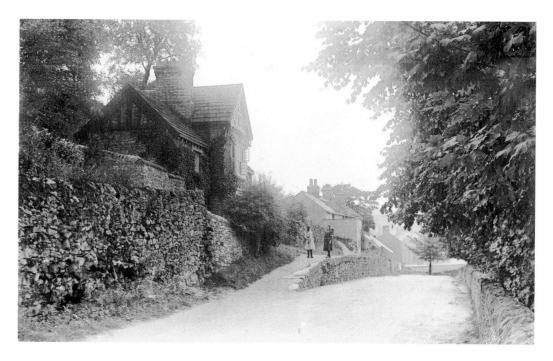

Swiss House, Dale End, Bradwell

This 1905 picture is of Swiss House at Dale End Bradwell which is now in a beautiful rural location. In the past Dale End was the site of lead mines and slag works. In April 1854 four men lost their lives at Slag Works, Dale End, suffocated by sulphurous fumes. Two of them, Elliott and Darnley, died trying to rescue their friends. One of those who died left behind a wife and two children and the other a wife and four children. There are few visible signs of any past industry today.

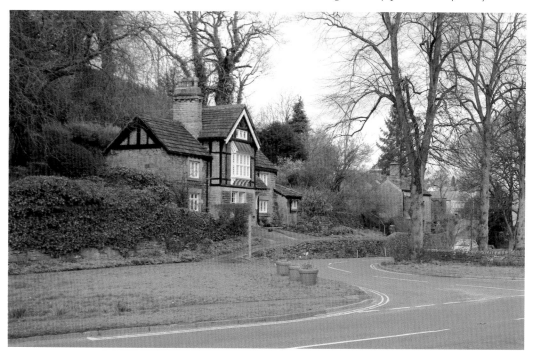

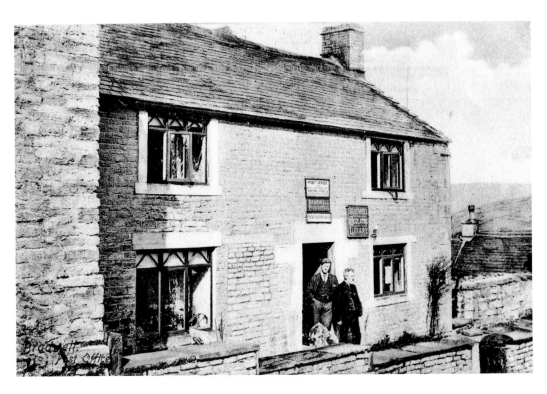

The Old Post Office, Smithy Hill, Bradwell
This photograph of the old post office on Smithy Hill was taken about 1920. The building is now a private residence.

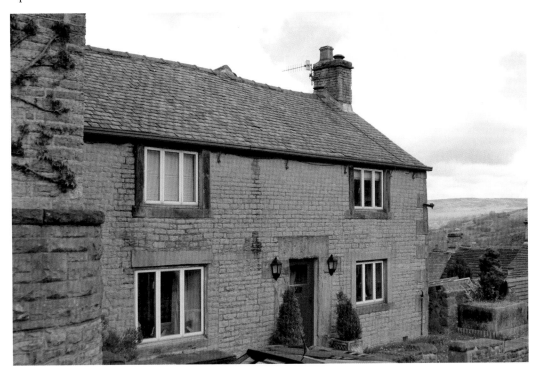

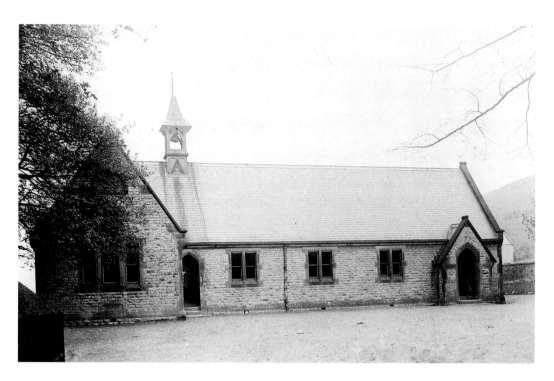

St Barnabas Church School

A School Board was formed in 1871 to organise the building of St Barnabas Church School which was built in 1872 for 110 children; with James Rowe as master and Miss Annie Miller Alexander as mistress. The exterior of the school has changed very little since except that the bell tower has been removed.

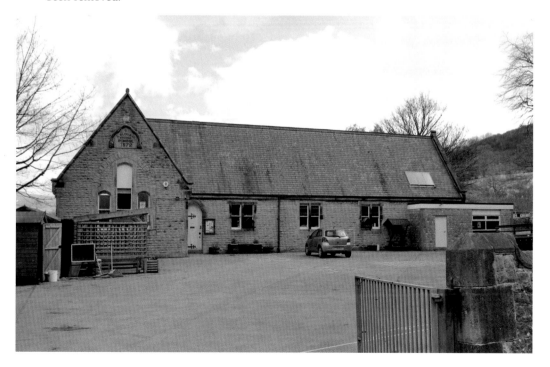

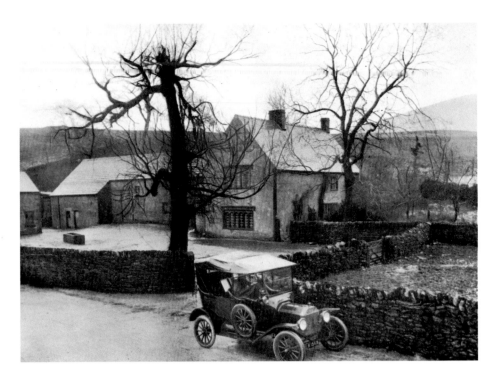

Hazlebadge Hall, Bradwell

This early 1900s photograph is of one of the earliest dwellings in Bradwell. Hazlebadge Hall dates from the Tudor period and has a date stone of 1549 above the coat of arms of the Vernon and Swynnerton families. Margaret Vernon was the last of the Vernon family, and it is said that she went insane after witnessing her lover's marriage to a rival at nearby Hope Church. Her ghost is said to haunt the hall and the nearby valley, with the occasional spectre of her galloping on a white horse at midnight between Hope and Hazlebadge Hall. The single wing that remains of the house is now part of a large farm complex.

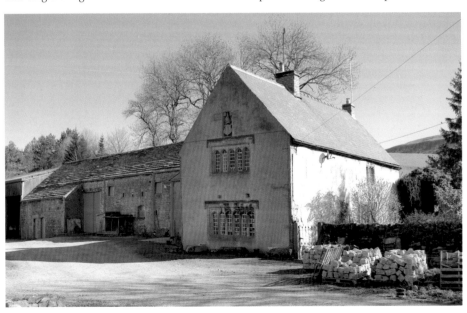

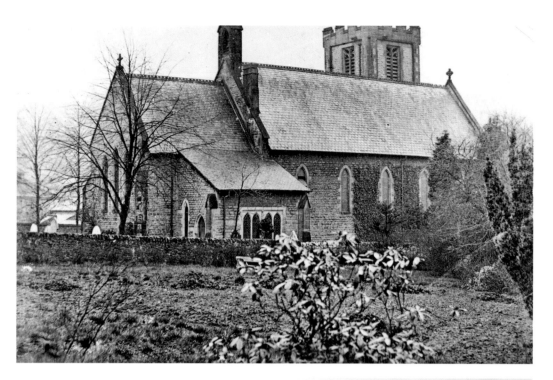

St Barnabas Church, Bradwell

This photograph is of St Barnabas Church in 1910. It was erected in 1868 and the tower added in 1888 at a cost of £1,004. A planned spire was never built. The clock in the tower was paid for by a local itinerant hawker known as 'Old Benny' (Benjamin Giles). Samuel Fox, a local businessman and industrialist from Bradwell, made a donation of £100 towards the cost of building the church. Fox, famous for developing the Paragon umbrella frame, also donated the land that became the churchyard and the vicarage. At the time of writing the church is undergoing extensive repairs.

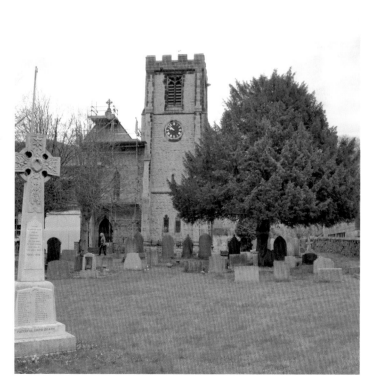

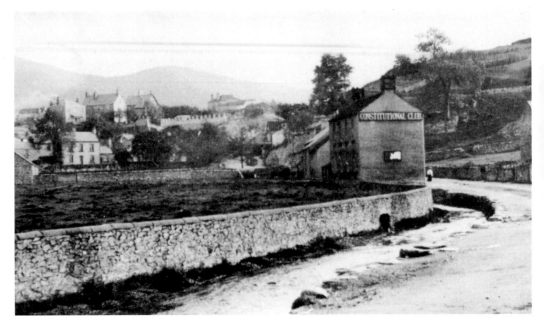

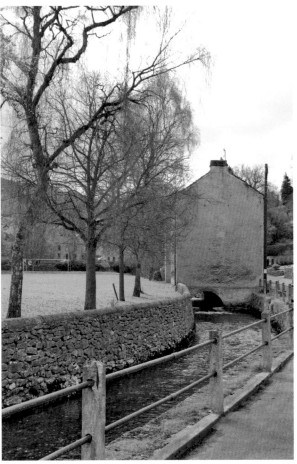

The Constitutional Club, Bradwell
This old photograph taken about 1913 shows an old mill which later became the Constitutional Club. A brook runs under the building. Today it is residential accommodation.

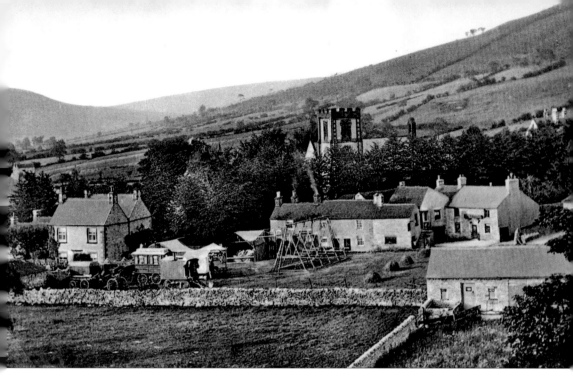

Recreational Grounds, Bradwell

This picture shows a travelling fair on a field near the old Shoulder of Mutton public house in 1904. Note the old swings and caravans. The building to the right is the old Shoulder of Mutton. St Barnabas Church can be seen the background.

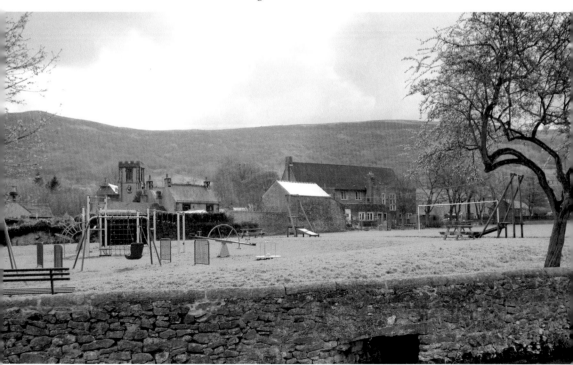

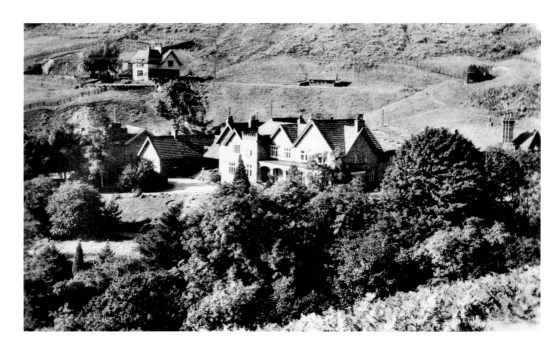

The Rowland Cote, Edale

This early twentieth-century photograph is of The Rowland Cote, Nether Booth, Edale. It was a hunting lodge but is now a YMCA hostel and Activity Centre. It is one of the best known walking and adventure locations in the country and offers activities such as caving, climbing, kayaking, canoeing, abseiling, orienteering and archery. Extra buildings have been added but the main building is substantially the same as in the earlier photograph.

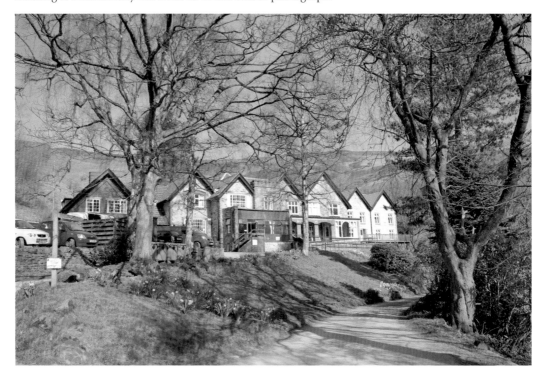

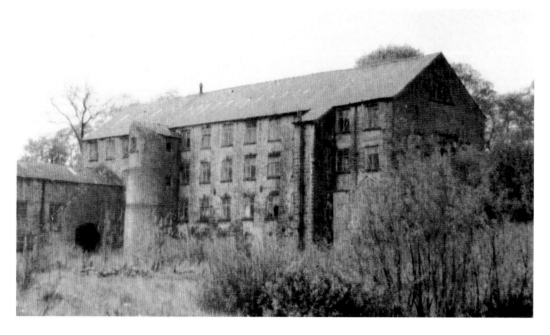

Edale Cotton Mill

This poor photograph is of Edale Cotton Mill in the 1940s when it was derelict. It was built in 1795 on the site of a corn mill. Workers were brought in from surrounding towns and accommodated in cottages nearby. Many of the women workers walked each day from Castleton over the thousand-foot Hollins Cross pass. Cotton continued to be produced at the mill until around 1940 but it then fell into disuse. It was restored in the early 1970s by the Landmark Trust. The building today is privately owned as the trust had to sell the lease to occupants.

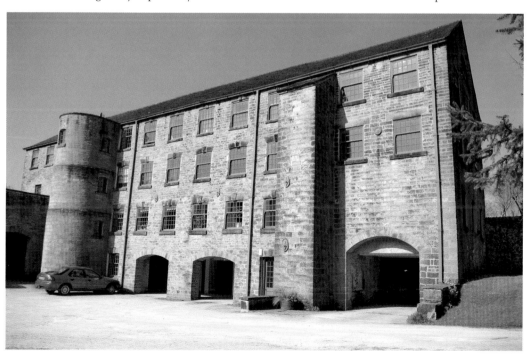

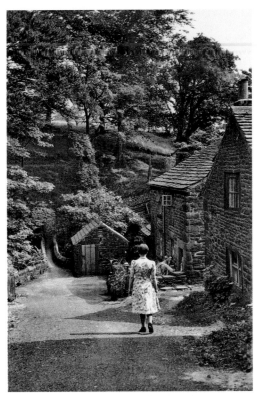

Grinds Brook Packhorse Bridge Edale
This 1950s photograph is of the old sixteenth-century packhorse bridge in Grinds Brook. The bridge is of stone construction but would only allow one traveller at a time to pass as it is so narrow. It is one of many early packhorse bridges in this area. It is today unchanged and is a most beautiful and historic part of the village of Edale.

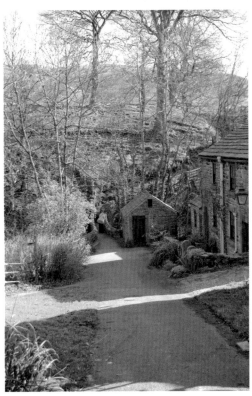

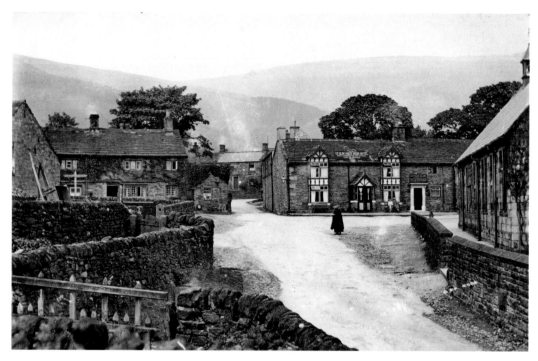

The Old Nag's Head Inn, Edale This late nineteenth-century photograph of the Old Nag's Head Inn, a former smithy dating back to 1577, is at the start of the Pennine Way walk. To the right of the picture is the local school which is still operating. The trackway to the right of this runs down to the old packhorse bridge at Grinds Brook.

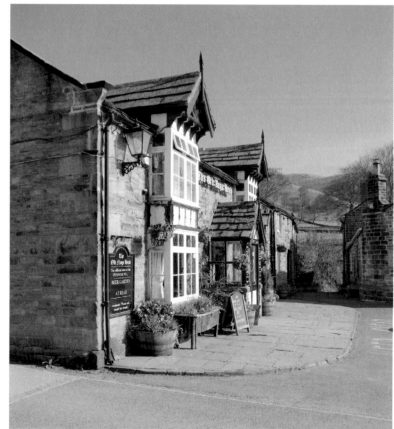

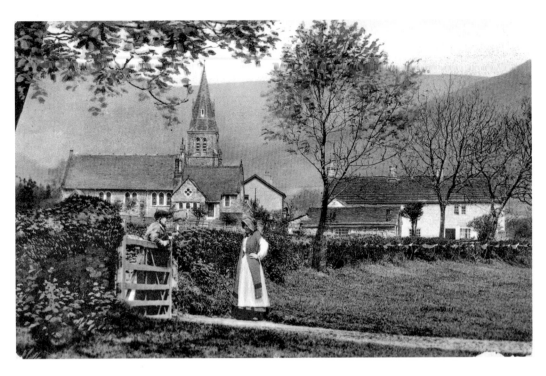

Edale Church

Edale Church was built in 1885, on the site of an earlier chapel. Before the present church was built, villagers were required to worship elsewhere and carry their dead for burial in neighbouring Castleton Church. Edale Church was designed by William Dawes of Manchester.

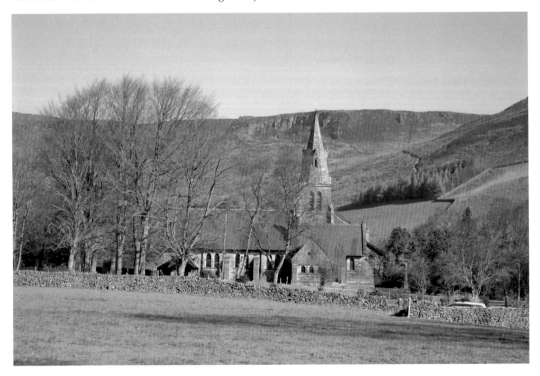

Barber Booth, Edale

Edale originally had no major settlement but had 'Booths'. These were shelters used in the fifteenth- and sixteenth-century by herdsmen tending cattle. Over time these shelters became permanent and then eventually areas where people lived. This is an early twentieth-century photograph of Barber Booth Edale showing the old packhorse bridge and the road leading to Castleton. On the left can be seen a Wesleyan chapel, built in 1811, which is illustrated in the modern photograph.

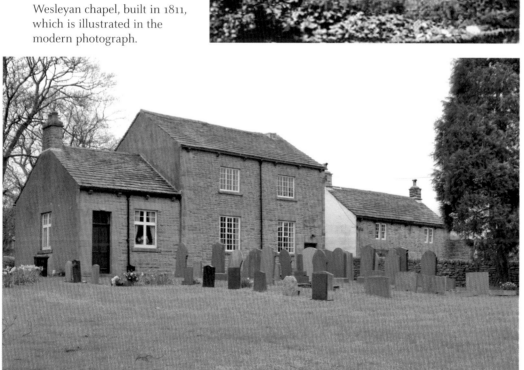

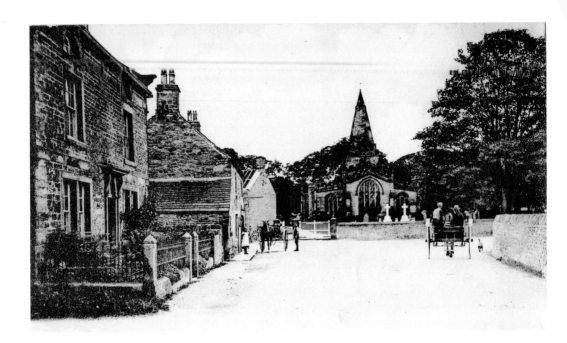

Hope Market Place

This view shows the east entrance to Hope Church in 1906. The house by the church gate, the vicar's house, is now long gone and the young girl is standing outside what is now a shop. The area to the east of the church was the old market place. The large house on the left is a 400-year old farmhouse which became a public house in 1720 known as the Cross Daggers Inn. The property was once owned by the Siddal family in the early 1800s. Lizzie Siddal married the Pre-Raphaelite painter Dante Gabriel Rossetti and was his model. Lizzie's father spent his fortune in the courts trying to prove ownership of the house. The Cross Daggers sign may have its origin in the fact that the Siddal family were cutlers in Sheffield.

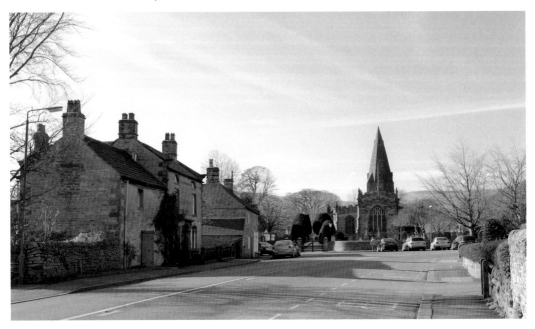

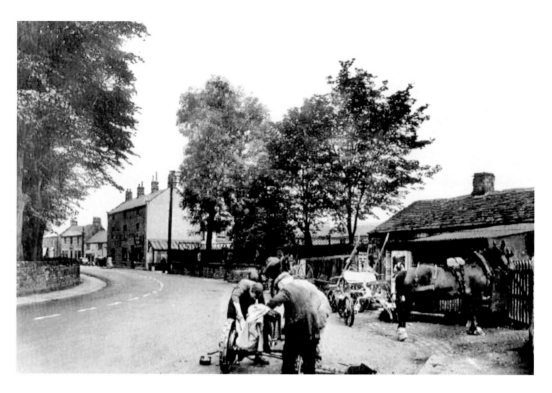

The Blacksmiths Hope

This photograph was taken in 1932 when Joseph Holmes & Sons were the Blacksmith's. The smithy was next to the cattle market which has been replaced by modern houses. The Old Hall Hotel can be seen in the distance. The gas lamps have disappeared from the roadside and a pathway has been made up by the churchyard wall.

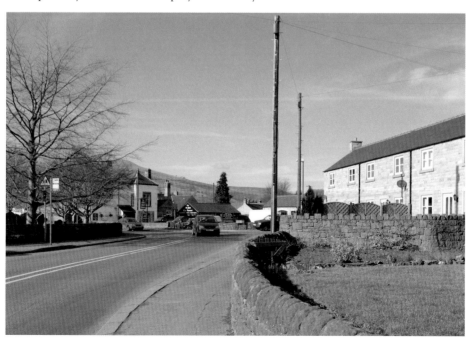

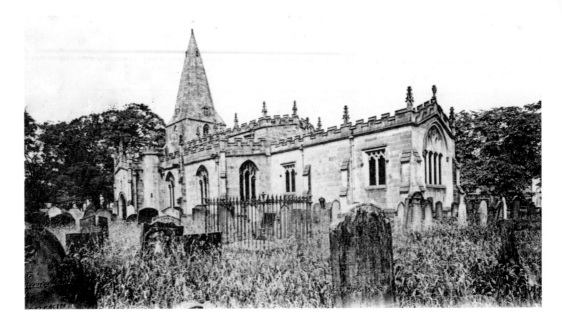

Hope Church

A Saxon church stood on this site before the present one which dates from the early 1200s. The present building dates mostly from the fourteenth century and was rebuilt in 1728 leaving only the west tower from the fourteenth-century period. In the churchyard stands a Saxon Cross and the repositioned old market cross. Hope Church records tell of the stealing of the body of twenty-eight-year-old William Bardwell on the night of 26 October 1831 and later on the night of 2 October 1834 twenty-one-year-old Benjamin Wragg's body was stolen by bodysnatchers.

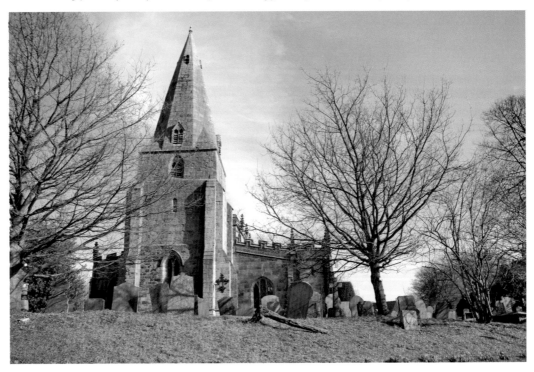

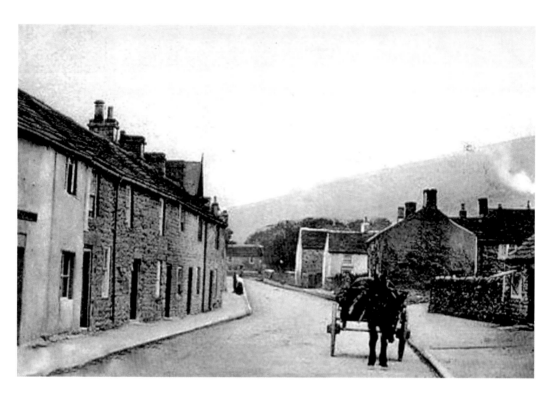

The Edale Road, Hope

Many roads in this village have been in use for hundreds of years. This road may be on the route of a very old highway called the Portway. This early twentieth-century scene looking north on the Edale road shows weavers' cottages, when sacking was woven, on the left hand side. The white lime-washed house on the right is Higher Hall originally an almshouse. The scene is very much the same today.

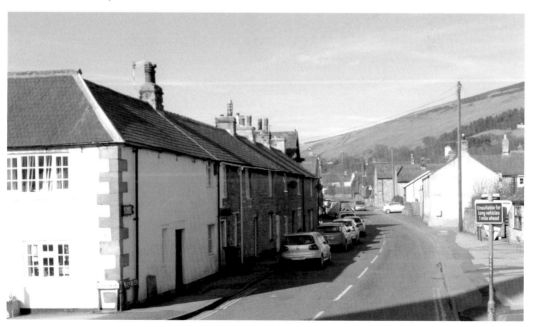

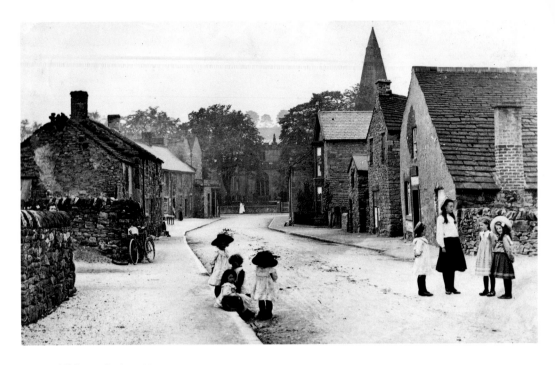

Children Playing, Hope

This is a late-1900s scene of the Edale Road looking south to the churchyard. This main road from Edale was not constructed until the 1850s. Children are playing but it is more likely that they have posed for this picture as they are in their best clothes. Notice that many of the buildings are built end on to the road. The white building on the left is a tin hut brought from Birchinlee, which is now a beautician's. Tin town was built to house the workers on the dams. It is one of the last surviving tin huts from Tin Town.

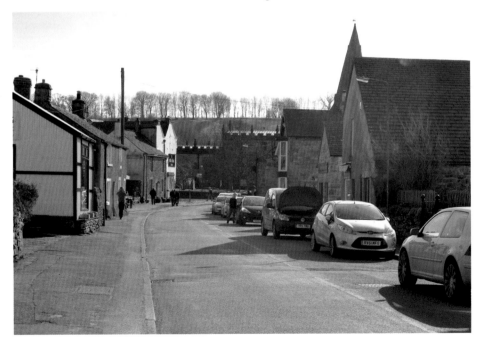

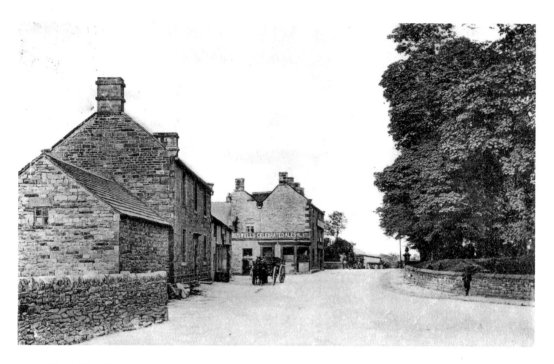

The Old Hall, Hope

This photograph shows the Old Hall Hope in 1905, first mentioned in 1272. It was remodelled in its present form in the 1500s and has been a public house or inn since the 1720s. To the right of the building can be seen the old smithy now demolished. The building on the left with a porch was the Durham Oxe Inn. Today it is the post office. The larger building is now the local supermarket. Notice the lack of footpaths apart from the narrow one by the churchyard wall.

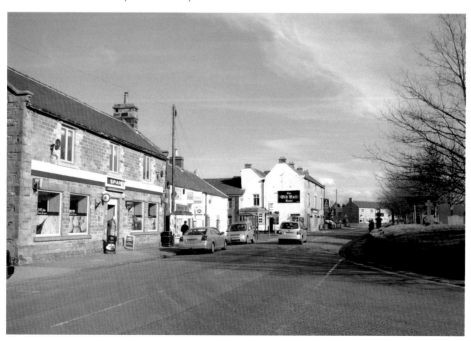

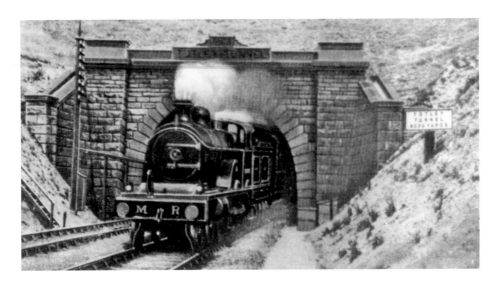

The Railways in the Hope Valley

The early photograph shows the first steam train through Totley Tunnel in 1894 when the main railway line was opened between Sheffield and Manchester. The line was being well used by the 1920s by commuters and holiday makers. The photograph below is of Hope Station staff in the early 1900s. By 1925 C. H. Thompson had been appointed to the post of station master. A year after his appointment in 1925 a fatal crash happened at the station in which three people died. The inset is a photograph of the train wreckage after that crash. Today the station is unmanned.

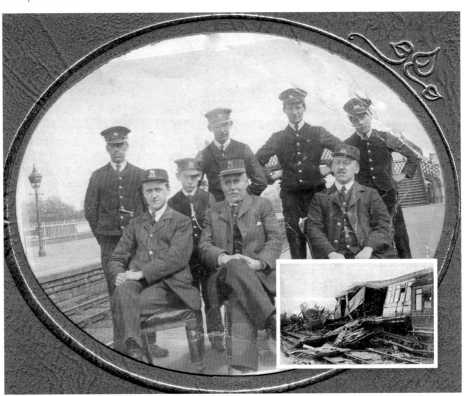

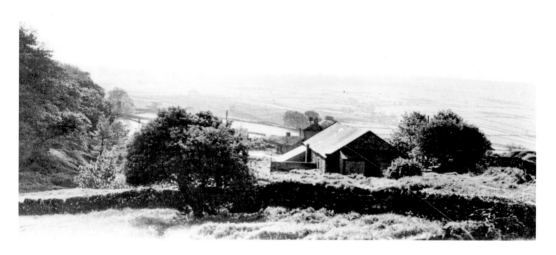

The Playhouse, Great Hucklow

The Playhouse at Great Hucklow was founded by L. Du Garde Peach who lived in the village. Peach was a great supporter of the amateur theatre and in 1927, he founded an amateur group in the village. It achieved a notably high standard and continued until 1971. In 1938 Great Hucklow created its own theatre by converting a cupola barn formally a building used for lead mining. Large audiences attended every production, consisting of visitors from all over the country. The early 1950s photograph shows the theatre. It is now the Foundry Adventure Centre.

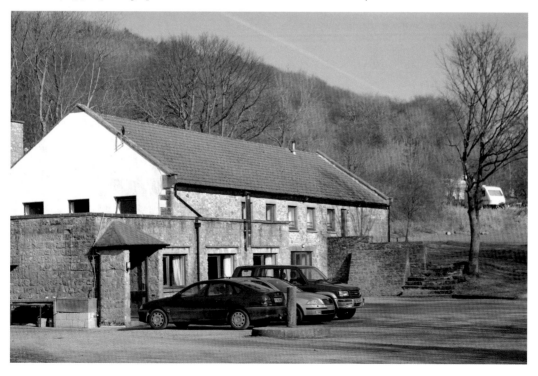

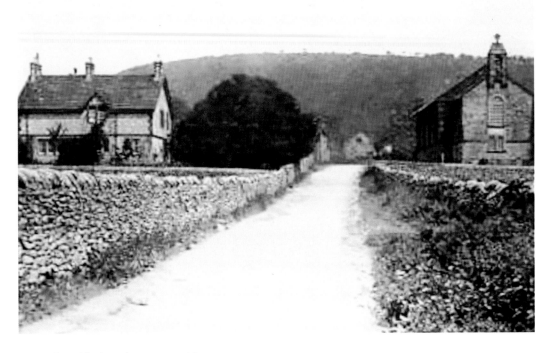

The Old Chapel, Great Hucklow

This photograph is of the Old Chapel in Great Hucklow, a Presbyterian establishment, founded in 1696 under the auspices of William Bagshaw, the nonconformist minister. The present building probably dates from 1797 when worship outside the Church of England was made legal. The present day congregation at this chapel is Unitarian, introduced in 1826. The house on the left was built in 1887 and functioned as a convalescent home at one time. Little has changed over the years.

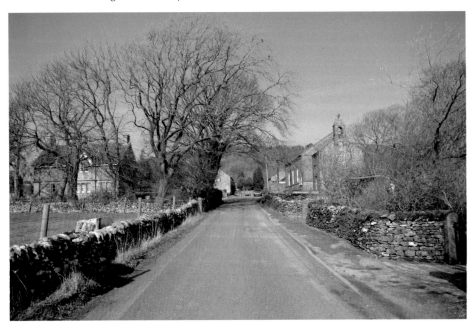

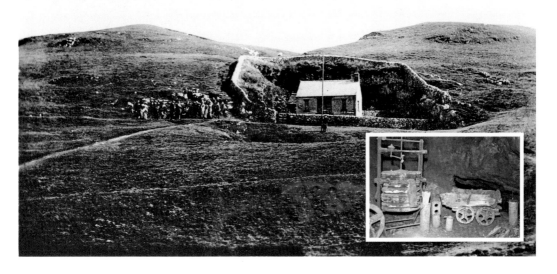

Blue John Cavern, Castleton

This photograph is of the Blue John Cavern in the early twentieth century. It is one of the four caves found in Castleton and takes its name from the mineral Blue John. This mineral is still mined in small amounts outside the tourist season and made locally into jewellery. The original lead miners' entrance was by a pothole which can be seen from inside the cavern. The first miners were lowered by rope down into the cavern. The inset is a photograph of some of the miners' tools used in the past.

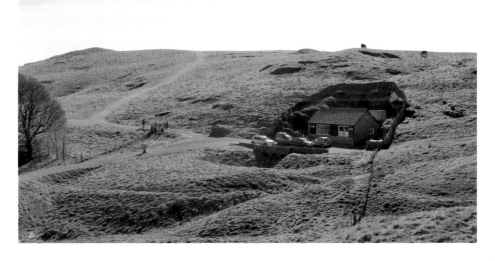

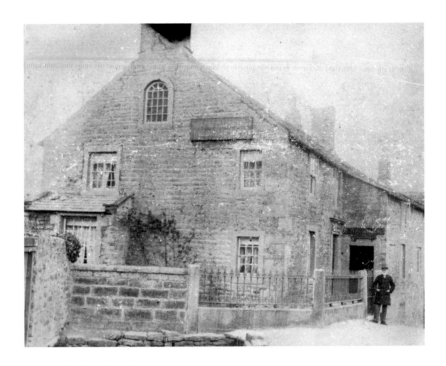

George Barber, Castleton

This late nineteenth-century photograph is of Mr George Barber outside his Tailor and Draper's establishment in Millbridge Castleton. George made suits for villagers and mill workers in Edale and at weekends walked to the mill in Edale to sell them. The building in Millbridge is now the Rambler's Rest a bed and breakfast establishment.

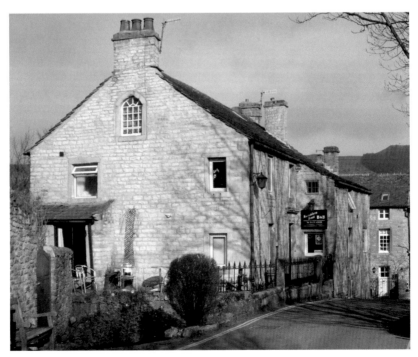

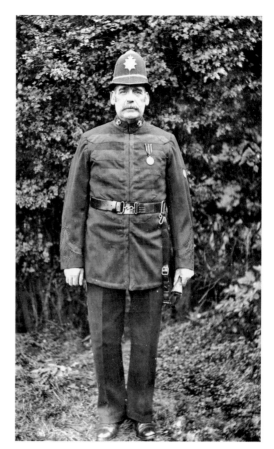

Policemen in Castleton
How uniforms and attitudes have changed over the years. The old late nineteenth-century photograph of a Castleton police constable can be compared with more relaxed attitude of the local sergeant in the mid 1900s. The sergeant seems to me mystified by the antics of the round the world unicyclist.

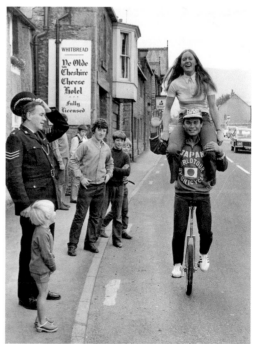

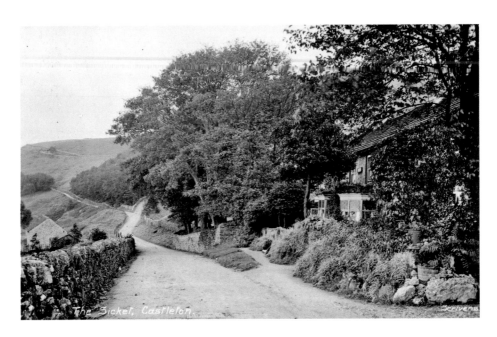

Old Cottage, Pindale Road, Castleton

This ancient rural track way out of Castleton leads to the hamlet of Pindale and on to Hope. The track to the right goes to Tideswell. This 1930s scene shows the old cottage built in the early 1600s. The cottage was awarded a conservation award from the Council for the Protection of Rural England in 2001 when it was renovated. The needle factory can be seen on the left of the picture, it is now a private residence. The public way which leads to this factory also leads on to the old Victorian rubbish dump, now disused.

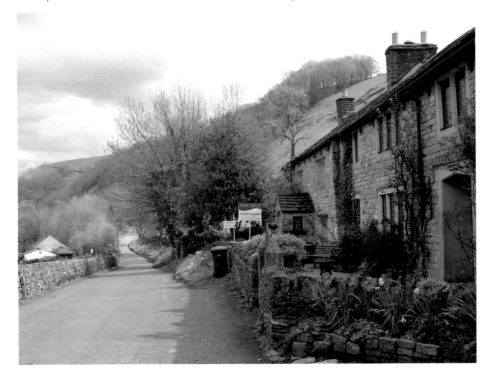

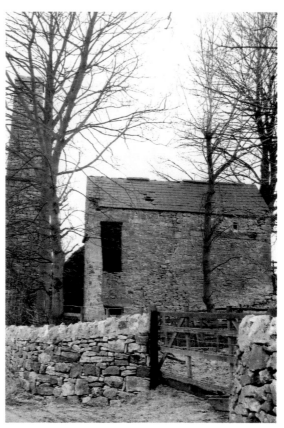

Lead Mine, Pindale

Lead mining was a very important industry in the Hope Valley. This mine built in 1742 was later owned by Robert How Ashton who had other mines and a lead smelting business in the locality in the 1800s. The old photograph taken in the 1940s is of the steam engine house of the Pindale lead mine. It was converted into a bunkhouse for walkers in 1988 as part of an outdoor centre. The inset is a picture of Robert How Ashton and his daughter in 1858.

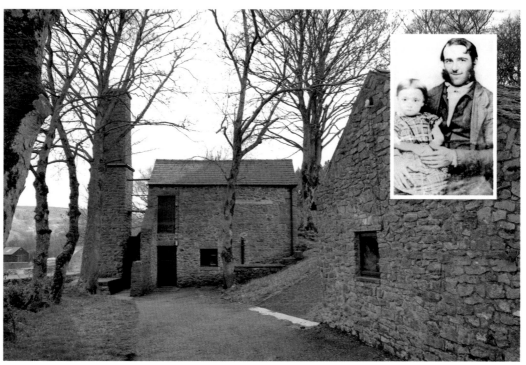

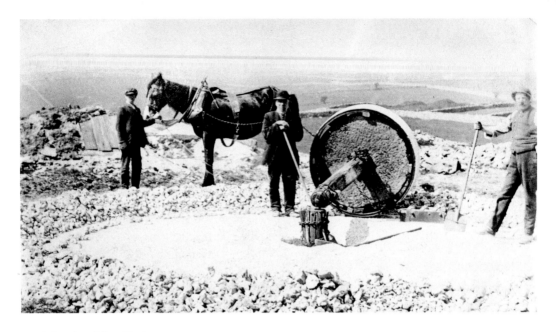

Lead Ore Crushing Circle

When lead ore was mined it had to be crushed to extract the lead and other minerals. They were usually operated by horses that drew the heavy metal rimmed wheel over the ore to crush and extract the minerals. The old photograph shows a working ore crushing circle in Bradwell in the early 1900s, once common in the Peak District. The modern photograph is of the crushing circle, associated with the Odin Mine at Castleton. It was operated in the early 1720s by at least seventeen women who dressed the ore taken from the mine. The circular stone was as usual worked by a horse.

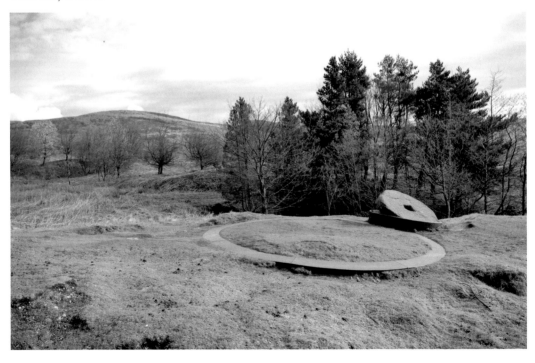

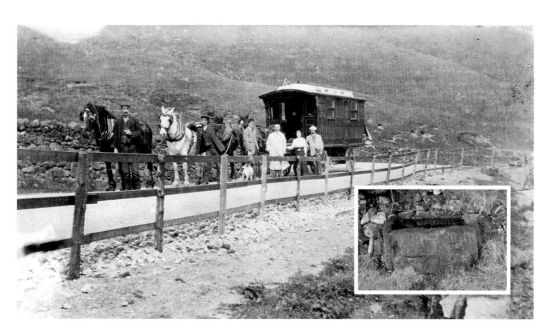

Early Tourism Hope Valley

Tourism has played a large part in the economy of the Hope Valley for hundreds of years. This photograph shows a holiday maker and his family trying to traverse the old turnpike road below Mam Tor, Castleton in May 1912. The party are being helped by local villagers who have loaned two horses to help them pull the caravan up the steep incline. The horses would have drank water from the stone trough on the roadside before attempting the long hard pull up the hill. The more modern mode of holiday transport is shown parked on the same road today, no longer a through road because of subsidence.

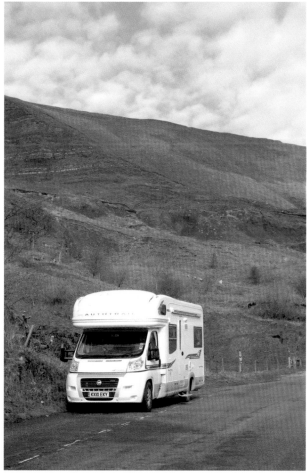

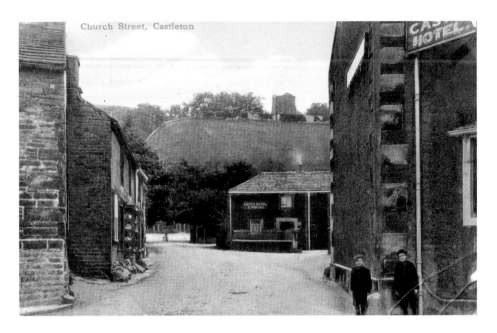

Castle Street, Castleton

This is a 1903 photograph of Castle Street, Castleton. It shows the Castle Hotel and its stables. Peveril Castle can be seen on the hill in the background. The modern photograph shows a busier scene. The stables are now hotel accommodation.

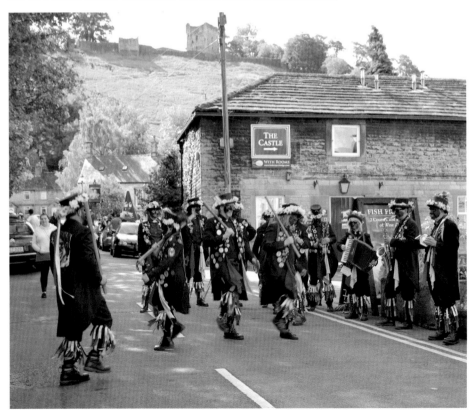

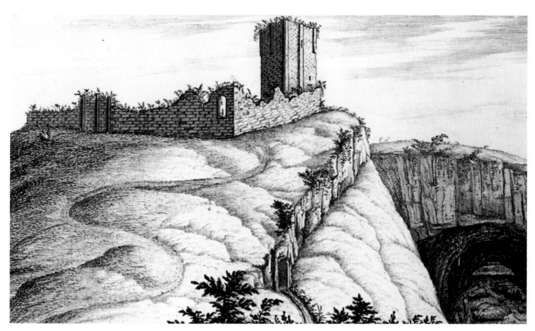

Peveril Castle Ruins

The ruins of Peveril Castle stand high above the village of Castleton. The castle is one of England's earliest Norman fortresses. William Peveril, who is thought to have been an illegitimate son of William, fortified the site of the present castle in 1080 and constructed a wooden keep, which was later converted into a stone building. The keep was built by Henry II in 1176.

The castle fell into disuse after Tudor times, and by the seventeenth century only the keep was in use as a courthouse. When this was abandoned, the castle gradually deteriorated until the remains were restored last century. Many of the cottages of local people were built from stone taken from the ruined castle.

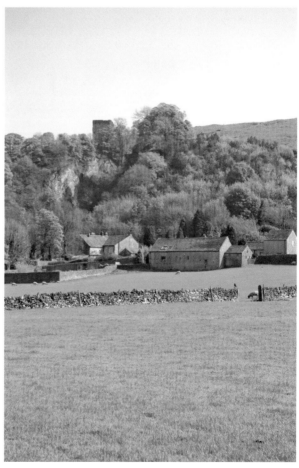

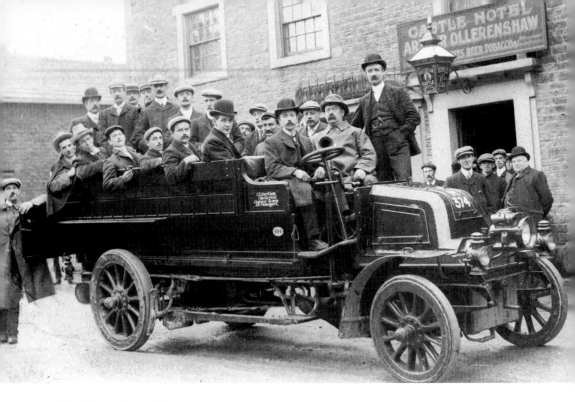

Tourism in the Hope Valley
A group of tourists taken to Castleton between 1901 and 1910 when Arthur Ollerenshaw was licensee of the Castle Hotel. The charabanc is owned by C. P. Markham, Chesterfield and was licensed to carry fifteen passengers.

Acknowledgements

This book has been accomplished with the goodwill and assistance of a number of people. Without my wife Jane, none of these books of projects I have undertaking in the past would have come to fruition. Much of the information in this book has been gained over the years from discussion with local people and historians. Thanks to all of them.

All the modern and the majority of old photographs are from the author's own collection acquired over a number of years. However the old photographs of Bamford were used with the permission of Mr Malcolm Dungworth of the Bamford History Society. He also gave me much valuable information on the history of the area and its buildings.